EVIDENCE: A STRUCTURED APPROACH

2006-2007 CASE, RULES, AND MATERIALS SUPPLEMENT

EVIDENCE: A STRUCTURED APPROACH

2006-2007 CASE, RULES, AND MATERIALS SUPPLEMENT

Featuring Side-by-Side Comparison of Federal Rules of Evidence and California Evidence Code

David P. Leonard
Victor J. Gold
Loyola Law School, Los Angeles

ASPEN
PUBLISHERS

76 Ninth Avenue, New York, NY 10011
http://lawschool.aspenpublishers.com

© 2006 Aspen Publishers, Inc.
a Wolters Kluwer business
http://lawschool.aspenpublishers.com

Aspen Publishers
Attn: Permissions Department
76 Ninth Avenue, Seventh Floor
New York, NY   10011

Printed in the United States of America.

1 2 3 4 5 6 7 8 9 0

ISBN 0-7355-6427-2

ISSN 1557-3818

About Aspen Publishers

Aspen Publishers, headquartered in New York City, is a leading information provider for attorneys, business professionals, and law students. Written by preeminent authorities, our products consist of analytical and practical information covering both U.S. and international topics. We publish in the full range of formats, including updated manuals, books, periodicals, CDs, and online products.

Our proprietary content is complemented by 2,500 legal databases, containing over 11 million documents, available through our Loislaw division. Aspen Publishers also offers a wide range of topical legal and business databases linked to Loislaw's primary material. Our mission is to provide accurate, timely, and authoritative content in easily accessible formats, supported by unmatched customer care.

To order any Aspen Publishers title, go to *www.aspenpublishers.com* or call 1-800-638-8437.

To reinstate your manual update service, call 1-800-638-8437.

For more information on Loislaw products, go to *www.loislaw.com* or call 1-800-364-2512.

For Customer Care issues, e-mail *CustomerCare@aspenpublishers.com*; call 1-800-234-1660; or fax 1-800-901-9075.

Aspen Publishers
a Wolters Kluwer business

CONTENTS

PREFACE

This volume has two purposes. First, it serves as a supplement to David P. Leonard & Victor J. Gold, *Evidence: A Structured Approach*. It updates the text with recent developments in evidence law, and also contains additions to the material.

The second purpose of the text is to present a side-by-side comparison of key features of the Federal Rules of Evidence and the California Evidence Code, arranged in the same order as in the textbook. In addition to the side-by-side comparison, we have added sets of "Questions for Classroom Discussion," which are designed to highlight the differences (and similarities) between these two codes. Students who plan to take the California Bar Examination should find these materials particularly useful, as the exam, beginning in 2007, will test both the Federal Rules of Evidence and the California Evidence Code.

Students should be sure to consult our textbook's website for downloadable copies of all sets of Questions for Classroom Discussion, as well as other update materials. The web address is: <http://faculty.lls.edu/structuredevidence/>.

David P. Leonard
Victor J. Gold

July 2006

Evidence: A Structured Approach

2006-2007 Case, Rules, and Materials Supplement

PART 1:
SUPPLEMENTARY MATERIAL

The materials in this part are designed to update and enhance the coverage of a number of subjects in *Evidence: A Structured Approach.*

The first major development since the publication of the text was the Supreme Court's decision in *Crawford v. Washington*, 541 U.S. 36 (2004). *Crawford* marks a new direction for the analysis of the relationship between the hearsay rule and the Sixth Amendment's Confrontation Clause. In 2006, the Court clarified the scope of *Crawford* in *Davis v. Washington*, 547 U.S. ___ (2006), 2006 WL 1667285.

The second important development concerns several amendments to the Federal Rules of Evidence that will take effect on December 1, 2006. Several changes to Rule 408, which governs the admissibility of compromise evidence, will clarify the reach of the rule's exclusionary principle and otherwise make the rule more understandable. An amendment to Rule 606(b) (juror testimony to impeach the verdict) would allow testimony that the verdict was the result of a clerical error. An amendment to Rule 609 (impeachment by prior conviction) would clarify the test for which crimes fit into the category of crimes "involving dishonesty or false statement." Finally, Rule 404(a) (character evidence offered to prove conduct) would be amended to make clear that the term "accused" applies only to a criminal defendant. The effect of this amendment would be to make clear that character evidence is never admissible to prove action in conformity. The effects of the amendments are discussed in Part 1. The amended versions of all four of these rules are presented in Part 2 of this Supplement.

In addition to reporting on recent developments, we have prepared a number of additional hypothetical transcripts of witness testimony. These help to illustrate how certain evidence rules are actually used, and how objections are made.

All updates and additional materials are keyed to the relevant sections and pages of *Evidence: A Structured Approach.*

CHAPTER
1

The Process of Proof

C. SOURCES OF EVIDENCE AND THE NATURE OF PROOF

2. *Witnesses: The Requirements of Competency, Personal Knowledge, and Oath or Affirmation*

b. Competency of Judge, Jurors, and Attorneys

Insert to p. 31:

An amendment to Rule 606 will go into effect on December 1, 2006. The purpose of the proposed amendment is to make clear that a juror may testify about "whether there was a mistake in entering the verdict onto the verdict form." The main purpose of the proposed amendment is to create a very narrow exception to allow a verdict to be impeached when the jury made an error in transcribing the verdict onto the verdict form; it would not allow juror testimony that the jurors misunderstood the court's instructions. The amendment does not deal with a number of other issues raised by the rule, including whether a juror may testify about threats or intimidation among members of the jury; whether the rule only bars juror testimony or affidavit to impeach the verdict, or also bars any testimony or affidavit from a non-juror (such as a court officer) who overhears or otherwise learns of the misconduct; and whether the rule only bars testimony or affidavit after the verdict has been announced.

3. *Real Evidence: Authentication and the Best Evidence Rule*

c. The Best Evidence Rule

Insert to p. 65:

Illustrating the best evidence rule. Application of the best evidence rule is relatively straightforward. Assume Plaintiff sues Defendant for negligence following an automobile accident. At trial, to prove the nature and extent of the damage to her car, Plaintiff calls Mechanic to the stand. After establishing that Mechanic worked on Plaintiff's car, the following takes place. "Pl" indicates Plaintiff's counsel; "Def" indicates Defendant's counsel.

Pl:	Please describe the nature of the damage to Plaintiff's car.
Mechanic:	The car suffered serious damage to the rear. The bumper was destroyed, as were the tail lights. The trunk was smashed and the back window was broken.
Pl:	Were you able to repair these parts?
Mechanic:	No. I had to replace all the parts I just mentioned.
Pl:	What was the total labor and materials cost for that work?
Mechanic:	I don't remember off the top of my head, but I have a photocopy of the invoice at my shop, and I looked at it before I came down here. I jotted down the total. It was …
Def:	Objection, Your Honor. The witness is not testifying from personal knowledge, but from the contents of a writing. This violates Rule 1002.
By the Court:	Objection sustained. Counsel, you'll have to bring in the invoice.
Pl:	I understand, Your Honor. My client does not have the actual invoice, but he does have a photocopy, and I would like to show that document to the witness. It has been marked for identification as Plaintiff's "A."
By the Court:	Go ahead, counsel.
Pl:	Let the record show that I have provided Defendant's counsel with a copy of this document. Mechanic, do you recognize this document?
Mechanic:	Yes. It's a copy of the invoice I sent to your client for the work done on the car.
Pl:	Do you always provide customers with such a document?
Mechanic:	Yes.
Pl:	Do you use the same form for all work?
Mechanic:	Yes. This is our standard form.
Pl:	Who prepares the invoice?
Mechanic:	My secretary prepares it from information supplied by the mechanic who does the actual work. I then review the invoice and we send it to the customer.
Pl:	Your Honor, we move the admission of Plaintiff's Exhibit "A."
By the Court:	The document will be marked as admitted into evidence.
Pl:	Please look at the document and tell the court what the total cost of the work was, including labor and materials.
Def:	Objection. This is not the original writing.
Pl:	Your Honor, this is a photocopy. A photocopy qualifies as a duplicate

	under Rule 1001(4). And under Rule 1003, it is admissible to the same extent as the original unless a genuine question has been raised about the authenticity of the original. No such question has been raised.
By the Court:	Objection overruled. The witness may read the total from the document.
Mechanic:	The total for the work, including labor and materials, was $4,512.34.
Pl:	No further questions.

In this example, Plaintiff's counsel successfully satisfied the requirements of the best evidence rule after it became clear that the witness did not have personal knowledge of the information sought. The source of proof was the invoice (actually, a photocopy of the invoice). For that reason, the best evidence rule was implicated. A photocopy of the invoice qualifies as a "duplicate," and is admissible to the same extent as the original. Thus, the court's ruling was correct. (Note, as well, that it was necessary to show that the invoice qualified as a business record. This is because the invoice constituted hearsay. In Chapter 3, we will discuss the hearsay rule and exceptions, including the exception for "regularly conducted activity," which includes businesses.)

Suppose that in this example, a fire had destroyed Mechanic's shop and all of his records, including the photocopy of the invoice. Assume as well that Defendant's counsel had asked Plaintiff to produce the invoice during discovery, that Plaintiff had done so, and that Defendant failed to bring the invoice to court after Plaintiff notified Defendant that she intended to use it to prove the damage to the car. In that case, Rule 1004(3) would allow Plaintiff to offer secondary evidence to prove the contents of the writing (the invoice). That evidence could consist of a number of things, including Plaintiff's testimony from memory about what the invoice said.

4.   *Judicial Notice*

a.   **Adjudicative Facts**

Insert to p. 71:

Illustrating judicial notice of adjudicative facts. Assume Plaintiff sues Defendant for negligence following a night-time collision between Defendant's car and Plaintiff's bicycle. The car struck Plaintiff from behind. Plaintiff admits she was wearing dark clothing, but claims Defendant should have seen her because the roadway was lit that night with bright moonlight. At trial, Defendant seeks to prove that the moon was not visible that evening. The colloquy might proceed as follows. "Pl" indicates Plaintiff's counsel; "Def" indicates Defendant's counsel.

Def:	I would ask the court to take judicial notice that on the evening in question, the moon was not visible because that night was a new moon, which cannot be seen.
Pl:	Objection, Your Honor. My opponent has not presented any data showing this to have been the case.
Def:	May I approach?
By the Court:	You may.
Def:	I have handed the bailiff a copy of a nationally circulated almanac for the year in which this accident took place. The court will find a yellow tag on the page showing the phases of the moon during the relevant month. The date on which the accident took place is denoted a new moon.
By the Court:	Any objection?
Pl:	May I see the almanac, Your Honor.
By the Court:	Will the bailiff please show counsel the book?
Pl:	Thank you, Your Honor. I withdraw the objection.
By the Court:	The court will take judicial notice that there was no visible moon on the night in question.
Def:	Would the court please instruct the jury accordingly?
By the Court:	The jury is instructed that there was no visible moon on the night in question. You must take that fact as true.

In this example, Defendant has done all that is necessary to require the court to take judicial notice. Under Rule 201(b), a fact may be judicially noticed if it is "not subject to reasonable dispute in that it is … (2) capable of accurate and ready determination by resort to sources whose accuracy cannot reasonably be questioned." Because the phases of the moon can be proven by the simple expedient of consulting an almanac, the fact qualifies for judicial notice. In addition, because Defendant has supplied the court with the almanac, the requirements of Rule 201(d) have been satisfied and the court must take judicial notice. Plaintiff has been given an opportunity to be heard according to Rule 201(e), and the court has instructed the jury according to the requirements of Rule 201(g).

CHAPTER
3

The Hearsay Rule

C.   THE HEARSAY RULE AND THE CONSTITUTION

3.   *Current Supreme Court Jurisprudence about the Relationship between Hearsay and the Confrontation Clause*

Insert to p. 300:

Just after the textbook was published, the Supreme Court took a sharp turn with its decision in *Crawford v. Washington*, 541 U.S. 36 (2004). Defendant Michael Crawford was charged with assault and attempted murder of Kenneth Lee, a man he believed had attempted to rape his wife Sylvia. The police interrogated Michael and Sylvia, and took tape-recorded statements from each. Michael Crawford's statement set forth facts supporting a self-defense claim. Sylvia's statement corroborated her husband's in a number of respects, but provided much weaker support for the self-defense claim. Sylvia did not testify at trial because of Washington's adverse spousal testimony privilege, which bars a spouse from testifying without the other spouse's consent. (For discussion of the spousal privileges, see Chapter 8.) Washington's privilege does not prevent the adverse party from offering into evidence a statement that satisfies a hearsay exception, however. Sylvia's statement was hearsay but qualified as a declaration against interest because she admitted leading her husband to Lee's apartment, which facilitated the assault. Over Michael's confrontation objection, the trial court allowed the prosecution to play the tape of Sylvia's statement to the jury, and Michael was convicted.

The United States Supreme Court held that admission of Sylvia's statement violated Michael's confrontation rights. Writing for a majority of seven, Justice Scalia reviewed the history of the confrontation right from Roman times to the present. Placing primary emphasis on the state of the common law at the time of the Sixth Amendment's framing, Scalia wrote:

> First, the principal evil at which the Confrontation Clause was directed was the civil-law mode of criminal procedure, and particularly its use of *ex parte* examinations as evidence against the accused....

> Accordingly, we once again reject the view that the Confrontation Clause applies of its own force only to in-court testimony, and that its application to out-of-court statements introduced at trial depends upon "the law of Evidence for the time

being." ... Leaving the regulation of out-of-court statements to the law of evidence would render the Confrontation Clause powerless to prevent even the most flagrant inquisitorial practices. Raleigh was, after all, perfectly free to confront those who read Cobham's confession in court....

The text of the Confrontation Clause reflects this focus. It applies to "witnesses" against the accused—in other words, those who "bear testimony." ... "Testimony," in turn, is typically "[a] solemn declaration or affirmation made for the purpose of establishing or proving some fact." ... An accuser who makes a formal statement to government officers bears testimony in a sense that a person who makes a casual remark to an acquaintance does not. The constitutional text, like the history underlying the common-law right of confrontation, thus reflects an especially acute concern with a specific type of out-of-court statement.

Id. at 50-52. Though the Court declined to provide a precise definition of "testimonial," it held that the category included, "at a minimum ... prior testimony at a preliminary hearing, before a grand jury or at a former trial; and to police interrogations." *Id.* at 68.

The Court held that "[t]he historical record ... supports [the] proposition that the Framers would not have allowed admission of testimonial statements of a witness who did not appear at trial unless he was unavailable to testify, and the defendant had a prior opportunity for cross-examination." *Id.* at 53-54. Thus, the Court established a bright-line rule for "testimonial" hearsay offered against a criminal defendant: Such hearsay is only admissible if (1) the declarant testifies at trial; or (2) the declarant is unavailable *and* the defendant had a prior opportunity to cross-examine the declarant. By so holding, the Court abolished the *Roberts* test in cases of "testimonial" hearsay. Under *Roberts*, trustworthy hearsay could be admitted where the declarant was unavailable, even if the hearsay was testimonial. After *Crawford*, even a high degree of trustworthiness does not satisfy the confrontation clause. The Court wrote that "[d]ispensing with confrontation because testimony is obviously reliable is akin to dispensing with jury trial because a defendant is obviously guilty." *Id.* at 62.

Crawford was a turning-point in the Court's confrontation clause jurisprudence. Now, even if hearsay fits within exceptions that admit "testimonial" statements, it will not be admissible against a criminal defendant unless the declarant testifies at the trial, or, if the declarant does not testify, she is unavailable to testify and the defendant had a prior opportunity for cross-examination.[1] This will certainly mean that grand jury testimony of a person who does not testify at trial will no longer be admissible against a criminal defendant because such statements are not subject to cross-examination. For the same reason, statements of individuals other than the criminal defendant, made during police interrogation, will not be admissible against the defendant. *Crawford* also casts doubt on

---

[1] The Court left open the possibility that statements satisfying the requirements of the dying declaration exception, even those that are "testimonial" in nature, might be admissible under the confrontation clause. *Id.* at 56 n.6. The Court pointed to historical evidence that the exception was the only one recognized in criminal cases at common law, and wrote that "[i]f this exception must be accepted on historical grounds, it is *sui generis.*" *Id.*

the validity of state child-hearsay exceptions, at least to the extent the child's statement is "testimonial" because it was made formally during police questioning.[2] At the same time, the results of many pre-*Crawford* cases will not change. To take the facts of *Roberts* itself, defendant had an opportunity to cross-examine the declarant at the preliminary hearing and the declarant was unavailable at the time of trial. Thus, the requirements of *Crawford* would have been satisfied.

When hearsay is not "testimonial," *Crawford* strongly suggests that the confrontation clause does not apply at all, and that the only barrier to admission is the hearsay rule. However, the facts before the Court in *Crawford* did not involve "non-testimonial" hearsay, so the case did not settle the matter clearly.

After the Supreme Court decided *Crawford*, the lower federal courts as well as state courts struggled to come to terms with the issues left open or only partially resolved by the Court. Among the many issues are the meaning of "testimonial"; the timing of the prior opportunity for cross-examination; the possibility that some hearsay exceptions (most notably the dying declaration exception) are *sui generis*, and thus not subject to confrontation analysis; and the relationship between forfeiture doctrine and the confrontation clause.

In June 2006, the Court revisited the confrontation issue in *Davis v. Washington*, 547 U.S. ___ (2006), 2006 WL 1667285. *Davis* considered the facts of two cases, one from Washington and the other from Indiana. In the Washington case, Michelle McCottry, Davis's former girlfriend, made a 911 call during which she claimed that Davis was present and "jumpin' on" her, using his fists. The 911 operator, whom the Court treated as an agent of law enforcement, ascertained certain other facts during the call, including McCottry's assertion that Davis had just left the scene, why Davis said he had come to McCottry's house, and Davis's full name and birth date. The police arrived within four minutes of the 911 call, saw that McCottry was shaken and had fresh bruises on her forearm and face, and noticed that McCottry was frantically trying to gather her belongings and children so she could leave. Davis was charged with violating a domestic no-contact order. At trial, the only witnesses against him were the two police officers who responded to the 911 call; McCottry did not testify. They testified about what they observed, but of course were unable to identify who caused McCottry's injuries. Over Davis's objection, key portions of the tape recording of the 911 call were admitted.

In the second case decided in *Davis*, police responded to a report of a domestic disturbance at the home of Hershel and Amy Hammon. When they arrived, the police saw Amy alone on the front porch. She appeared frightened but said nothing was wrong.

---

[2] Note how the decision in *Crawford* affects the way the Court would treat Lilly v. Virginia, 527 U.S. 116 (1999) (discussed in the text at pp. 297-300). The result—exclusion of the evidence—would not change, but the analysis would be quite different. The statement of Mark Lilly (defendant's brother) was "testimonial" because it was made during police interrogation, as in *Crawford*. Because defendant did not have an opportunity to cross-examine Mark, the statement would plainly be inadmissible, regardless of whether the hearsay exception under which it was admitted is "firmly rooted."

She gave the officers permission to search the house, where the officers observed a gas heating unit with flames coming out of the front. Broken glass was on the floor in front of the unit. Hershel was in the kitchen, and told police that he and Amy had had an argument, that the argument had not gotten physical, and that everything was fine. One of the officers then took Amy aside and asked her what had happened. The other officer restrained Hershel from joining that conversation. After listening to Amy's story, the officer asked her to fill out and sign a "battery affidavit." She handwrote the document, stating that Hershel had broken the furnace, shoved her down on the floor into the broken glass, hit her in the chest, thrown her down, and broken other items. She also asserted that Hershel "tore up my van where I couldn't leave the house" and attacked her daughter. Hershel was charged with domestic battery and probation violation and tried at a bench trial. Amy was subpoenaed to appear at trial, but failed to do so. The state called the officer who had questioned Amy and asked him to recount what she told him and to authenticate the affidavit. Over Hershel's objection, the court then admitted the affidavit as a "present sense impression" and Amy's statements as "excited utterances." The judge convicted Hershel.

With Justice Scalia writing for an 8-1 majority, the Supreme Court held that the tape of the 911 call was not testimonial and thus was properly admitted in Davis's trial. It held, however, that the Indiana court erred in admitting the affidavit against Hammon. Because the statements in both cases were made in the context of interrogation by police officers or their agents,[3] the Court began its analysis with an effort to determine what statements made to law enforcement are "testimonial" in nature:

> Without attempting to produce an exhaustive classification of all conceivable statements—or even all conceivable statements in response to police interrogation—as either testimonial or nontestimonial, it suffices to decide the present cases to hold as follows: Statements are nontestimonial when made in the course of police interrogation under circumstances objectively indicating that the primary purpose of the interrogation is to enable police assistance to meet an ongoing emergency. They are testimonial when the circumstances objectively indicate that there is no such ongoing emergency, and that the primary purpose of the interrogation is to establish or prove past events potentially relevant to later criminal prosecution.[4]

The key feature of this holding is the objective nature of the test. Statements are nontestimonial when the "circumstances objectively indicat[e] that the primary purpose of the interrogation is to enable the police to meet an ongoing emergency." They are testimonial when "the primary purpose of the interrogation is to establish or prove past events potentially relevant to later criminal prosecution."

---

[3] The Court considered the 911 operator in *Davis* to be an agent of law enforcement even if not a police officer herself.

[4] In a footnote, the Court stressed that although the statements at issue in these cases were both made during police interrogation, "[t]his is not to imply ... that statements made in the absence of any interrogation are necessarily nontestimonial."

The Court next held that the Confrontation Clause applies only to "testimonial" hearsay. Citing early state confrontation cases, the Court noted that each involved testimony of one kind or another. Indeed, the Court stated, "[w]ell into the 20th century, our own Confrontation Clause jurisprudence was carefully applied only in the testimonial context." Though some more recent cases had muddied the waters, the right to confrontation attaches only to such statements:

> When we said in *Crawford* ... that "interrogations by law enforcement officers fall squarely within [the] class" of testimonial hearsay, we had immediately in mind (for that was the case before us) interrogations solely directed at establishing the facts of a past crime, in order to identify (or provide evidence to convict) the perpetrator. The product of such interrogation, whether reduced to a writing signed by the declarant or embedded in the memory (and perhaps notes) of the interrogating officer, is testimonial."

A 911 call, the Court held, does not meet this definition because the "call ... and at least the initial interrogation conducted in connection with a 911 call, is ordinarily not designed primarily to 'establish[h] or prov[e]' some past fact, but to describe current circumstances requiring police assistance." Thus, it differs from the interrogation in *Crawford* because it concerned "events *as they were actually happening*," and that any reasonable listener would recognize that the caller was describing an ongoing emergency rather than past events. In addition, "the nature of what was asked and answered in *Davis*, again viewed objectively, was such that the elicited statements were necessary to be able to *resolve* the present emergency, rather than simply to learn (as in *Crawford*), what had happened in the past." Finally, the Court noted "the difference in the level of formality" between the interviews in *Crawford* and *Davis*. Apparently, the more formal the interview, the more likely the hearsay is "testimonial." Concluding, the Court wrote that McCottry "simply was not acting as a *witness*; she was not *testifying*. What she said was not 'a weaker substitute for live testimony' at trial," as was the testimony in *Inadi* (discussed in the text).[5]

The Court then turned to *Hammon*, which it considered an easier case because the statements were similar to those in *Crawford*: "It is entirely clear from the circumstances that the interrogation was part of an investigation into possibly criminal past conduct .... There was no emergency in progress .... Objectively viewed, the primary, if not indeed the sole, purpose of the interrogation was to investigate a possible crime." Even though the *Crawford* interrogation was more formal, the interview in *Hammon* was sufficiently similar to be considered testimonial:

---

[5] The Court recognized that a 911 call that begins in a nontestimonial context can become testimonial once the need for emergency assistance has ended. In *Davis*, for example, after the 911 operator learned what she needed to address the emergency and Davis had left the premises, the answers McCottry gave to the operator's questions were most likely testimonial, "not unlike the 'structured police questioning' that occurred in *Crawford*." Trial courts should redact any testimonial hearsay through *in limine* procedures.

Both declarants were actively separated from the defendant.... Both statements deliberately recounted, in response to police questioning, how potentially criminal past events began and progressed. And both took place some time after the events described were over. Such statements under official interrogation are an obvious substitute for live testimony, because they do precisely *what a witness does* on direct examination; they are inherently testimonial.

The Court was careful to note that its holding does not mean that questioning on the scene of alleged crime will never yield nontestimonial answers. Officers called to investigate domestic disputes need to learn who they are dealing with so they can assess the situation, including any possible threats to their own safety or to that of the victim. Thus, "[s]uch exigencies may *often* mean that 'initial inquiries' produce nontestimonial statements." But this was not the case in *Hammon*, "where Amy's statements were neither a cry for help nor the provision of information enabling officers immediately to end a threatening situation."

Finally, the Court took note of the availability of forfeiture doctrine to deal with situations in which a domestic violence victim is intimidated or coerced into refusing to testify. When this occurs, the Confrontation Clause might appear to grant a "windfall" to the guilty, but

the Sixth Amendment does not require courts to acquiesce. While defendants have no duty to assist the State in proving their guilt, they *do* have the duty to refrain from acting in ways that destroy the integrity of the criminal-trial system. We reiterate what we said in *Crawford*: that "the rule of forfeiture by wrongdoing ... extinguishes confrontation claims on essentially equitable grounds." ... That is, one who obtains the absence of a witness by wrongdoing forfeits the constitutional right to confrontation.

On remand in *Hammon*, the Indiana courts might be asked to determine whether defendant forfeited his right to the protection of the Confrontation Clause.

Davis helps to clarify the broad scope of the Court's new confrontation jurisprudence. For example, the Court has now made clear what it implied in *Crawford*: that the Confrontation Clause does not apply to "nontestimonial" hearsay. This holding clears the way for admission of any "nontestimonial" hearsay that satisfies a hearsay exception. The Court has also forged a rough test for determining when hearsay fits within one category or the other: The key is whether the declarant was acting in a manner similar to a trial witness. If the statement was made to police, the trial court should consider whether it was given to help police deal with an ongoing emergency (nontestimonial) or whether it was part of an investigation into past events (testimonial). The more formal the questioning, the more likely the declarant's statements are testimonial. And trial courts should be aware that the character of statements can change, requiring careful redaction of inadmissible parts. Much remains to be clarified, of course, but it is reasonable to guess that the Supreme Court will leave most such clarification to the state and lower federal courts.

A prominent law professor whose theories were cited by the Supreme Court in *Crawford*, and who was appointed counsel to Hammon in the Supreme Court, maintains a blog devoted to the Confrontation Clause: http://confrontationright.blogspot.com/.

Questions for Classroom Discussion
Casebook Page 301

1. Prosecution of Bob for bank robbery. Alice, an alleged accomplice, told police while under interrogation that she was the mastermind of the crime but that Bob was also involved. Alice died while in custody. Would admission of Alice's statement against Bob violate the Confrontation Clause?

2. Same case. While in jail, Alice made the same statement to Sally, her cellmate. Unknown to Alice, Sally was a police officer who was posing as a prisoner. Would admission of Alice's statement violate the Confrontation Clause?

3. Prosecution of Dennis for the shooting murder of Victim on a street corner. Dennis claims he was just in the wrong place at the wrong time, and that the killing had been committed by another person. At trial, the prosecution calls Wilma to testify that she arrived at the intersection moments after the collision and saw Walker kneeling next to Victim, sobbing. If permitted, Wilma will next testify that Walker suddenly pointed to Dennis and screamed, "You did it!" Walker died before the trial. Would admission of the declarant's statement violate the Confrontation Clause?

CHAPTER
4

Evidence of Character, Uncharged Misconduct, and Similar Events

2. *Character Evidence Offered for Non-Credibility Purposes*

B. **CHARACTER EVIDENCE**

e. **Proving Character as Circumstantial Evidence of Out-of-Court Conduct**

Insert to p. 331:

On December 1, 2006, an amendment to Rule 404(a) will make clear that the exceptions created in the rule apply only in criminal cases. (This would resolve once and for all the meaning of the word "accused" in the rule.) The Advisory Committee Note to the amendment states that "[t]he Rule has been amended to clarify that in a civil case evidence of a person's character is never admissible to prove that the person acted in conformity with the character trait."

Insert to p. 342:

Illustrating the basic rules. The following transcript illustrates how parties might use some of the basic rules governing the use of character evidence to prove a person's out-of-court conduct. Doug is prosecuted for assault and battery on Vic. Assume that during the prosecution's case-in-chief, Vic testified that he and Doug were coaches of opposing kids' soccer teams, and that they got into an argument during a game about a referee's call. Vic testifies that Doug suddenly became violent and struck Vic on the head with the edge of a clipboard, inflicting a severe cut.

As part of Doug's defense, defense counsel calls Wilma, a parent whose child was on Vic's soccer team. "Pros" indicates the prosecutor; "Def" indicates defense counsel.

Def:	Do you know Vic?
Wilma:	Yes.
Def:	How long have you known him?
Wilma:	About two years.
Def:	And how do you know him?
Wilma:	For the last couple of years, my son has played on soccer teams, and Vic has been his coach both years.
Def:	In the course of those two soccer seasons, did you have occasion to observe Vic's behavior?
Wilma:	Sure. I always go to the games.
Def:	And do you have an opinion about whether Vic is a peaceful or violent person?
Wilma:	Yes. I think Vic is easily angered and tends to be pretty violent at times.
Def:	Thank you. No further questions.
By the Court:	Cross-examination?
Pros:	Thank you, Your Honor. Wilma, have you ever heard of an organization called "Talk First"?
Wilma:	Yes.
Pros:	And what is the purpose of that organization?
Wilma:	I think it promotes non-violent solutions to disputes.
Pros:	Did you know that Vic received that organization's "Talker of the Year" award last year?
Def:	Objection. This is not proper rebuttal.
Pros:	This is similar to evidence of specific instances of conduct, which are allowed under Rule 405(a)
By the Court:	I'll allow it. It's not exactly the typical sort of specific instance of conduct, but I think it reflects peaceful conduct. Objection overruled. The witness will answer the question.
Wilma:	No, I hadn't heard that.
Pros:	Do you know Doug?
Wilma:	Not personally, but we live in the neighborhood and our kids have been involved in sports together for a few years.

Pros:	Do you ever hear people speak about Doug's character for peacefulness?
Wilma:	I suppose I hear some things.
Pros:	Did you ever hear that Doug threatened to punch a referee during a soccer game last year?
Wilma:	No, I never heard such a thing.
Pros:	Thank you. Your Honor, I have no further questions.

Defense counsel then calls Walker to the witness stand.

Def:	Are you familiar with Doug, the defendant in this case?
Walker:	Yes.
Def:	How do you know Doug?
Walker:	We work together at the auto parts plant in town.
Def:	How long have you worked together?
Walker:	About three years.
Def:	Do you work in the same part of the plant?
Walker:	Yes. I first met Doug when I started to work on the engine line. He was already on that line, and he's been there with me ever since.
Def:	Have you had occasion to observe Doug's behavior with his co-workers?
Walker:	Yes.
Def:	And do you have an opinion about Doug's character for peacefulness?
Walker:	Yes. I think he's a real peacemaker around the plant. He often breaks up fights and I've never seen him get involved in one.
Pros:	Your Honor. I move to strike the last part of the witness's answer as a violation of Rule 405(a).
By the Court:	Motion granted. The jury will ignore everything the witness said after describing Doug as a peacemaker.
Def:	No further questions, Your Honor.
By the Court:	Cross-examination?
Pros:	Did you know that several months ago, Doug was reprimanded for roughing up a work-mate following a dispute?
Def:	Your Honor, I object. May we approach?
By the Court:	Counsel will approach.

Def:	This is the first I've heard of such an incident. The prosecutor has to have some proof that it occurred.
Pros:	Your Honor, I have interviewed the victim of this attack and am prepared to bring him in if you would like to hear from him.
Def:	Your Honor, I've looked at Doug's personnel file, and there's nothing about this incident.
Pros:	That's because the employer agreed to make this an informal reprimand. It won't go in the defendant's personnel file.
By the Court:	Objection overruled. I'll allow the question.
Pros:	Will the court reporter please read back the question?
	[The court reporter reads back the question.]
Walker:	No. I didn't know of such an incident.
Pros:	No further questions.
Def:	Just one question, Your Honor.
By the Court:	Go ahead, counsel.
Def:	If your son was assigned to play soccer on Doug's team, would you have any problem with that?
Pros:	I object, Your Honor. This goes beyond allowable limits under the character evidence rules.
Def:	It does not, Your Honor. I am only seeking to demonstrate the witness's opinion more fully. I am not asking the witness to relate any specific instances of conduct.
By the Court:	Objection overruled. You may answer the question, Walker.
Walker:	I'd have no problem if my kid were assigned to Doug's team.
Def:	Thank you. I have no further questions.

In this example, the prosecutor did not offer any evidence of defendant's character during its case-in-chief, nor would the rules have allowed the prosecution to do so under these circumstances. Doug's first witness, Wilma, was a character witness. Rule 404(a)(2) allows the defendant in a criminal case to present evidence of a pertinent trait of the victim's character. Peacefulness is a pertinent character trait, and Wilma probably knows Vic well enough to have an opinion about Vic's character for peacefulness. Rule 405(a) limits character evidence on direct examination to reputation and opinion. This was opinion. On cross-examination, the prosecutor sought to rebut the inference of Vic's violent character. The prosecutor did so by asking Wilma about Vic's receipt of an award for promoting non-violence. Rule 405(a) allows the use of specific instances of conduct on cross-examination of a character witness. Although receipt of an award is not exactly a specific instance of conduct, the court's ruling on defendant's objection was probably correct. Receipt of an award of this kind can be seen as circumstantial evidence of a specific instance or instances of conduct. In fact, it can also be seen as circumstantial evidence of the organization's opinion that Vic is a peaceful person.

The prosecutor then continued the cross-examination of Wilma by eliciting evidence of defendant's violent character. A recent amendment to Rule 404(a)(1) allows the prosecutor to respond to the defendant's presentation of character evidence concerning the victim with evidence concerning the same trait of character in the defendant. That was the prosecutor's intent at this point. The prosecutor's questions sought testimony about Doug's reputation, and the witness appears to have been qualified to offer such testimony.

Doug's next witness was Walker, who was a typical character witness. Walker appears to have been sufficiently familiar with Doug to present an opinion about Doug's character for peacefulness. (Observation of Doug in a work setting over a period of three years is probably sufficient.) Defense counsel sought Walker's opinion, but after offering it, Walker backed up the opinion with evidence of specific instances of conduct (stating that Doug often breaks up fights and doesn't get involved in fights himself). The prosecutor's motion to strike the last part of the answer was proper because the answer went beyond the allowable form of character testimony during direct examination. Thus, the court's ruling striking the last part of Walker's answer was correct. The prosecutor's cross-examination of Walker was also proper, as long as the prosecutor had a good faith belief that the event inquired about actually occurred. That was the purpose of the colloquy at sidebar. The court's ruling appears correct; the prosecutor has shown a good faith basis for believing that the event actually took place.

Doug's brief redirect examination was probably also proper. Asking the witness whether he would allow his kid to play soccer on a team coached by Doug appears to be a further explanation of the basis of her opinion that Doug is a peaceful person.

CHAPTER
5

Exclusion of Other Relevant Evidence
for Reasons of Policy

C.   COMPROMISE AND PAYMENT OF MEDICAL AND SIMILAR EXPENSES

Insert to p. 392:

Several amendments to Rule 408 will go into effect on December 1, 2006. These amendments will address three important and longstanding conflicts about the admissibility of statements made during the course of compromise negotiations.

The first amendment will clarify Rule 408 to state that the rule excludes "conduct or statements made in compromise negotiations" whether offered in civil or criminal cases. It creates a narrow exception, however, for situations in which the settlement conduct took place in the context of "negotiations related to a claim by a public office or agency in the exercise of regulatory, investigative, or enforcement authority." In those situations, evidence of the settlement conduct may be admitted in a subsequent criminal case. When the settlement negotiations took place in run-of-the-mill civil litigation, evidence of those negotiations is inadmissible in both civil and criminal matters.

The second proposed amendment would clarify the scope of the "impeachment" use of compromise evidence. There is conflicting case law concerning whether compromise evidence is only admissible to prove "bias or prejudice of a witness" (one of the specific purposes currently listed in the rule), or may be admitted also to impeach by contradiction or prior inconsistent statement. The Advisory Committee proposes to amend the first part of the rule to make clear that compromise evidence is not admissible "to impeach through a prior inconsistent statement or contradiction." (The last part of the rule would continue to list witness bias as a permissible use of compromise evidence.)

The third proposed amendment would make clear that compromise statements and offers are excluded whether offered against or by the party who made the statement or offer.

The proposed amendment also reorganizes the rule to make it easier to read and apply. As part of its effort in this respect, the Advisory Committee proposes eliminating the sentence, "This rule does not require the exclusion of any evidence otherwise discoverable merely because it is presented in the course of compromise negotiations."

CHAPTER
6

Examining Witnesses; Attacking and Supporting the Credibility of Witnesses

E.   WITNESS CHARACTER

4.   *Conviction of Crime*

Insert to p. 448:

Two amendments to Rule 609 will go into effect on December 1, 2006. These amendments are intended to clarify certain matters about the types of crimes admissible to impeach a witness's character for truthfulness.

The amendment will make two changes. First, by changing the first sentence of subdivision (a)(1) to read, "For the purpose of attacking the character for truthfulness of a witness," the rule would allow the use of criminal convictions only to impeach a witness's *character for truthfulness*, not for other types of impeachment. Second, subdivision (a)(2) will be amended by changing the phrase "evidence that any witness has been convicted of a crime shall be admitted if it involved dishonesty or false statement…" to "evidence that any witness has been convicted of a crime that readily can be determined to have been a crime of dishonesty or false statement shall be admitted…." This amendment is intended to resolve a conflict among the courts over how to determine whether a conviction was of a crime involving dishonesty or false statement. Some courts look only to the elements of the convicted crime. Others consider any available information that helps determine whether the witness committed an act of dishonesty or false statement either before or after committing the crime. The Advisory Committee was persuaded by the Justice Department that a crime should qualify for automatic admission under subdivision (a)(2) even if its elements do not require deceit, and the Judicial Conference agreed. On the other hand, the "readily can be determined" language in the proposed amendment means that the trial court should not conduct a mini-trial to determine whether the witness committed a deceitful act while committing a crime.

The amendment will leave certain questions unresolved. One question is exactly what is meant by the phrase "that readily can be determined." What documents or other proof would be permitted? The amendment does not answer this question fully. Another remaining issue concerns the interaction of Rules 608 and 609. If a person has been convicted of a crime, may the conviction be admitted under Rule 609 and evidence of the underlying conduct admitted under Rule 608? Or is the use of Rule 608 barred whenever the witness has been convicted of a crime arising out of the underlying conduct? The answer to this question is unclear under the current rule, and the amendment does not clarify the matter.

H.   PRIOR STATEMENTS OF WITNESSES

Insert to p. 482:

3.   *Illustrating the Use of Prior Consistent and Inconsistent Statements*

Defendant is charged with the murder of Vic during a botched attempt to rob the Springfield branch of First State Bank. Defendant claims she was not involved, and intends to call an alibi witness.

At trial, the prosecution calls Will. After establishing that Will works as a teller at the bank, the following colloquy takes place. "Def" indicates defense attorney; "Pros" indicates the prosecutor.

Pros:	Where were you during the early afternoon of May 2 of last year?
Will:	I was at work at the bank.
Pros:	Do you remember what happened at approximately 2:30?
Will:	Yes. Someone entered the bank and attempted to rob the teller who was stationed next to me.
Pros:	Did you have an opportunity to see the robber clearly?
Will:	Yes.
Pros:	How close were you to the robber during this time?
Will:	Maybe 6 or 8 feet.
Pros:	Was the robber male or female?
Will:	Female.
Pros:	Please describe the robber's appearance.
Will:	She was average height and had very short dark brown hair and brown eyes. She appeared to be Caucasian.
Pros:	What clothes was the robber wearing?
Will:	She was wearing a light-colored raincoat and long pants.
Pros:	[The prosecutor questions the witness further concerning the robbery, and then concludes.] I have no further questions for this witness, Your Honor.
By the Court:	Cross-examination?

Def:	Thank you, Your Honor. Will, do you recall a conversation with Ward, the bank manager, on the day after the robbery?
Will:	Yes.
Def:	During that conversation, didn't you say that the robber was wearing dark sunglasses?
Pros:	Objection. Calls for hearsay.
Def:	No, Your Honor. I am trying to establish the witness's inconsistency. I do not intend to offer the witness's prior statement to prove its truth.
Pros:	The statement, even if made, would not be inconsistent with the witness's direct examination testimony. She said nothing about sunglasses, one way or the other.
Def:	The witness testified that the robber had brown eyes. If the robber was wearing dark sunglasses, the witness could not have determined the robber's eye color.
By the Court:	Objection overruled. The witness will answer the question.
Will:	I don't remember saying that.
Def:	And didn't you describe the robber as tall?
Will:	I did not.
Def:	Nothing further, Your Honor.
Pros:	Just a couple of questions. Will, do you recall a conversation with a police detective at the bank just a few minutes after the robbery?
Will:	Yes. We were all told to stay there until the detective had a chance to interview us.
Pros:	And during that interview, did you describe the color of the robber's eyes?
Will:	Yes. I said the robber had brown eyes.
Def:	Move to strike. This is hearsay.
Pros:	Not hearsay, Your Honor. This is a prior consistent statement.
By the Court:	Motion to strike granted. The jury will disregard the question and answer.
Pros:	Nothing further, Your Honor.

After the prosecution rests, defense counsel calls Ward, the bank manager.

Def:	What do you do for a living?
Ward:	I am the manager of the Springfield branch of First State Bank.

Def:	Do you recall a conversation with Will on May 3, the day after the robbery?
Ward:	Yes. I remember the conversation.
Def:	During that conversation, did Will describe what the robber was wearing?
Ward:	Yes.
Def:	Did Will say whether the robber was wearing sunglasses?
Pros:	I renew my earlier hearsay objection, Your Honor.
Def:	I'm only impeaching, Your Honor. This is not hearsay.
By the Court:	Objection overruled.
Ward:	Yes. Will told me the robber was wearing dark sunglasses.
Def:	Did will say anything about the robber's eye color?
Ward:	No.
Def:	And did Will say anything about the robber's height?
Ward:	Yes. He said the robber was tall.
Pros:	Would the court please instruct the jury about the limited admissibility of this testimony?
By the Court:	Members of the jury. You are not to consider this witness's testimony about what Will said as any evidence concerning the appearance of the robber, including whether the robber was wearing sunglasses and the robber's height. You may consider this testimony only insofar as it tends to affect the witness's credibility.
Def:	Nothing further, Your Honor.
By the Court:	Cross-examination?
Pros:	No questions, Your Honor.

In this example, the prosecutor has elicited Will's testimony that the robber had brown eyes. On cross-examination, defense counsel asks Will whether he made a statement to the bank manager the next day that the robber was wearing dark sunglasses. Though not inconsistent on its face, such a statement is inconsistent in the sense that it is doubtful the witness could have determined the robber's eye color if the robber was wearing dark glasses. The prosecutor's objection that the question calls for hearsay is invalid because defense counsel is not trying to prove the robber was wearing dark glasses, but only that the witness said so, that the statement is inconsistent with the witness's direct examination testimony, and that therefore, the witness should not be believed. Of course, the witness denies making the statement, which means that at this point, there is no evidence of the prior inconsistent statement. (The lawyer's question is not testimony.)

Later during the cross-examination, defense counsel also seeks to elicit Will's admission that during the same conversation the day after the robbery, he told the bank manager that the robber was tall. Again, Will denies making the statement.

On redirect examination, the prosecutor hopes to rehabilitate Will's credibility by demonstrating that very shortly after the robbery, Will told a police officer that the robber had brown eyes. This is a prior *consistent* statement because it is consistent with Will's direct examination testimony. Prior consistent statements are governed by Rule 801(d)(1)(B). To be admissible, the declarant must testify at the trial or hearing, be subject to cross-examination concerning the statement, and the statement must be offered to "rebut an express or implied charge of recent fabrication or improper influence or motive." This last requirement is not met. Defendant is not claiming that Will fabricated his trial testimony or otherwise had a motive to testify that he robber had brown eyes. Thus, the statement is not admissible. The trial judge correctly sustained defense counsel's objection.

Defense counsel then calls Ward for the purpose of proving the prior inconsistent statements that Will denied making. This constitutes extrinsic evidence of the statement because the proof is coming through another witness, not through Will during his cross-examination. Thus, Rule 613 is implicated. That rule requires that extrinsic evidence of a prior consistent statement may not be offered unless the declarant has an opportunity to explain the statement or deny making it. Because defense counsel already confronted Will with the statement during his cross-examination, that requirement has been satisfied. Thus, it is proper to call Ward to establish the making of the statement. For the same reasons, defense counsel may also establish that Will told Ward the robber was tall.

Note that Will's prior inconsistent statements are not admissible to prove the truth of the matters asserted (that the robber was wearing dark glasses and that she was tall). This is because the statements were not made under circumstances that satisfy the requirements of Rule 801(d)(1)(A). Specifically, to be admissible under that rule, a prior inconsistent statement must have been "given under oath subject to the penalty of perjury at a trial, hearing, or other proceeding, or in a deposition." This was not the case. Will was simply speaking with his manager. The prosecutor acted properly in requesting the court to instruct the jury as to the limited admissibility of the prior inconsistent statements, and the court's instruction was valid.

CHAPTER
7

Lay and Expert Opinion Evidence

B.   LAY OPINION

Insert to p. 497:

Illustrating the lay opinion rule. Plaintiff sues Defendant for negligence after Defendant's black SUV struck Plaintiff as Plaintiff crossed Evergreen Street between First and Second Avenues. This was in a residential neighborhood. Plaintiff claims Defendant was driving at excessive speed through the neighborhood, sped around a corner, and was not able to stop in time to avoid striking Plaintiff. At trial, Plaintiff calls Wyn, and the following colloquy takes place. "Pl" indicates Plaintiff's counsel; "Def" indicates Defendant's counsel.

Pl:	Ms. Wyn, where were you at 12:15 p.m. on June 4 of last year?
Wyn:	I was on my daily run. I was on Evergreen, headed east.
Pl:	Were you on the street?
Wyn:	Yes. I was running along the left side of the street, close to the curb.
Pl:	Were you approaching a cross street at that time?
Wyn:	Yes. I was about half-way between First and Second Streets, heading toward Second.
Pl:	Was the road ahead of you straight?
Wyn:	No. The road made a fairly sharp turn from the left ahead of me, about a half block past the Second Street intersection.
Pl:	Did you notice a black SUV at that time?
Wyn:	Yes.
Pl:	In what direction was it heading?
Wyn:	The SUV was heading west, so it was coming my way.
Pl:	What drew your attention to the SUV?
Wyn:	Well, I was looking straight ahead, so cars coming toward me along Evergreen were in my range of vision.
Pl:	Okay. Did other cars come into your range of vision at about that

	time?
Wyn:	There might have been a few. I don't really remember
Pl:	So what caused you to pay attention to the black SUV?
Wyn:	Well, first I noticed it because I heard screeching brakes, so I focused on the road ahead and saw this black SUV.
Pl:	Was the screeching sound you mentioned caused by that vehicle?
Def:	Objection, Your Honor. Lack of foundation for the opinion.
Pl:	Your Honor, with the court's permission, I will lay the foundation.
By the Court:	Go ahead.
Pl:	Were you able to tell what caused this screeching sound?
Wyn:	It was clearly a car. I know the sound of screeching brakes when I hear it.
Pl:	Were you able to determine which vehicle made the sound?
Wyn:	Yes.
Pl:	Which vehicle made the sound?
Def:	Your Honor, I renew my objection. Though I am sure the witness can testify that a sound was caused by a vehicle's screeching brakes, as the record stands counsel has not shown how the witness could have determined which vehicle made the noise.
Pl:	This witness is perfectly capable of stating that, Your Honor.
By the Court:	I do not believe you have shown how the proposed testimony will be rationally based on the witness's perception. I'm going to sustain the objection.
Pl:	May I continue with this line of questions, Your Honor? I would like another opportunity to make the showing.
By the Court:	I'll allow a few more questions.
Pl:	Thank you, Your Honor. Ms. Wyn, were you looking at any vehicles when you heard the sound.
Wyn:	I don't remember. I just remember hearing a screeching sound and then focusing on this SUV rounding the bend.
Pl:	Let's move ahead. Did the SUV pass you?
Wyn:	Yes.
Pl:	Can you estimate the SUV's speed when it passed you?
Def:	Objection. Lacks foundation for an opinion.
Pl:	Your Honor, the witness is perfectly capable of estimating the speed

	of a moving vehicle. This is a matter of common experience, and the witness had a sufficient opportunity to make the necessary observation.
By the Court:	I'll allow it. Objection overruled.
Def:	May I be heard, Your Honor?
By the Court:	Go ahead.
Def:	If the witness intends to state an actual speed in miles per hour, I think that is not rationally based on her perception. First, she was not in another moving vehicle and so could not use her own speedometer as a reference point. Second, she was running in the opposite direction of my client's vehicle. It is very difficult to estimate speed under those circumstances.
Pl:	Your Honor, as I said, this is a matter of common experience.
By the Court:	I'll allow the witness to estimate within ranges, but not a specific speed.
Pl:	Ms. Wyn, is it your opinion that the SUV was moving faster or slower than 25 miles per hour?
Wyn:	Definitely faster.
Pl:	Was it faster than 40 miles per hour?
Wyn:	Yes.
Pl:	Faster than 60?
Wyn:	I don't think so.
Pl:	I have no further questions for this witness, Your Honor.

In this example, Plaintiff's counsel seeks to elicit several opinions from the witness. Because Wyn is a lay witness, Rule 701 applies. That rule limits lay opinions to those which are (1) rationally based on the perceptions of the witness; (2) helpful to a clear understanding of the witness's testimony or in determining a fact in issue; and (3) not based on specialized knowledge (expertise). *First*, the witness gave an opinion that the screeching sound came from a person applying the brakes on a vehicle. Note that defense counsel did not object to this opinion. Most likely this opinion is permissible. A lay witness has sufficient experience to interpret the sound of screeching tires caused by hard application of a vehicle's brakes. The opinion is helpful to the jury because it would be very difficult to explain facts alone and give the fact-finder a sufficiently complete picture of what the witness actually perceived.

Second, Plaintiff's counsel hoped to be permitted to elicit Wyn's opinion that the sound issued from the SUV, which other evidence shows was Defendant's vehicle. The problem here is that it does not appear that Wyn actually saw the vehicle as it was making the sound. If the SUV was the only vehicle in the area from which the sound came, perhaps the opinion would be rationally based on the witness's perception. But Plaintiff's counsel did not develop that information either at first or after defense counsel objected. This example also can be viewed as one that implicates the personal knowledge rule (Rule 602). Arguably, the problem here was that Wyn lacked the kind of sensory perception necessary to give her personal knowledge of the source of the sound. Whether based on the opinion rule or the personal knowledge rule, the court acted properly in sustaining Defendant's counsel's objection.

Third, Plaintiff's counsel wanted to have Wyn testify how fast the SUV was traveling. This is a close case. Certainly, there are situations in which a lay witness may testify about the speed of a vehicle. If, for example, the witness was traveling in another vehicle alongside the one at issue, and if the witness knew the speed of her own vehicle, a court probably would allow her to offer an opinion as to the speed of the other car (even if the two were traveling at somewhat different speeds). Here, however, Wyn was running in one direction and the SUV was traveling toward her. It is much more difficult to say that Wyn's estimate of the vehicle's speed in such a situation is rationally based on her perception. Most likely, an opinion would be unduly speculative. Certainly, a court would be acting well within its discretion if it disallows the opinion. Note, however, that Plaintiff's counsel did not give up. The court allowed counsel to elicit the speed of the vehicle within a rough range. This is much more likely to be rationally based on the Wyn's perception, and though the result might not have been as useful to Plaintiff's case as a specific opinion as to speed, the testimony still gives Plaintiff's counsel something from which to argue at the close of the case. (Note, in addition, that even had the court allowed Wyn to state a more specific opinion about the vehicle's speed, defense counsel might have been able to undercut the opinion fairly substantially during cross-examination by showing that it was not truly based on the Wyn's perceptions.)

C. EXPERT OPINION

8. *Expert Testimony Must Have Proper Basis*

Insert to p. 524:

Illustrating the permissible bases of expert opinions. Following a fire that destroyed her commercial building, Plaintiff made a claim on her fire insurance policy. The insurer refused to pay, however, claiming that the fire was set deliberately, and that Plaintiff was responsible. Plaintiff has sued the insurer to require it to make payment on the policy. At trial, the insurer's counsel calls Inspector Fox, a county fire inspector who investigated the fire. After establishing Fox's expert credentials and eliciting Fox's opinion that the fire was set deliberately, the following colloquy takes place. "Def" indicates counsel for the Defendant insurance company; "Pl" indicates Plaintiff's counsel.

Def:	Inspector Fox, why did you conclude that the fire was set intentionally?

Fox:	I followed guidelines set by the National Fire Protection Association.
Def:	What is this organization?
Fox:	The NFPA is dedicated to reducing the effects of fires on quality of life. It does so by providing and advocating scientifically-based consensus codes and standards, research, training, and education.
Def:	Does NFPA have inspection standards for determining the origins of fires?
Fox:	Yes. Those standards are always evolving, of course, but there is a set of standards currently in place.
Def:	Where can those standards be found?
Fox:	They are published in NFPA 21, which is called the Guide for Fire and Explosion Investigations. It came out in 1998.
Def:	May I approach, Your Honor?
By the Court:	Yes.
Def:	Can you identify the document I am now showing you?
Fox:	Yes. This is a copy of NFPA 21.
Def:	Your Honor, prior to trial, I supplied a copy of this document to Plaintiff's counsel.
By the Court:	Proceed with your examination, counsel.
Def:	Did you follow those standards in your inspection of this fire?
Fox:	Yes.
Def:	How did you conduct the investigation, then?
Fox:	My first step was to examine the scene. We always try to arrive as quickly as possible after the fire has been extinguished, before the scene has been altered in any way.
Def:	When did you begin your inspection in this case?
Fox:	I arrived just after the fire was out.
Def:	Had anyone else been through the building before you, other than the firefighters who were involved in extinguishing the fire? .
Fox:	Not to my knowledge.
Def:	What did your inspection show?
Fox:	I always look for traces of accelerant, and I found some in this case.
Def:	What is an accelerant?
Fox:	It is a substance used to cause the fire to spread quickly.

Def:	What accelerant did you find in this case?
Fox:	I found traces of kerosene, which is a common accelerant used by arsonists.
Def:	Where did you find the traces of kerosene?
Fox:	In northeast corner of the first floor.
	[Counsel then takes the witness through a detailed description of his examination of the remains of the building.]
Def:	Other than your personal inspection of the building's remains, did you rely on anything else in reaching your conclusion that this fire was deliberately set?
Fox:	I interviewed several neighbors who were present just as the fire broke out.
Def:	And what did these people tell you?
Pl:	Objection, Your Honor. Calls for hearsay and improper basis for an expert's opinion.
Def:	If the Court will permit, I will demonstrate that experts in this field rely on the statements of witnesses when conducting investigations of this kind. And we will not be using those statements to prove the truth of the matters stated by the witnesses, but only to demonstrate the basis of Inspector Fox's opinion.
By the Court:	Objection overruled.
Def:	Inspector Fox, is it proper procedure for fire inspectors to interview percipient witnesses when seeking to determine the cause of a fire?
Fox:	Yes. We consider direct observations about the places were smoke was first seen, the color of flames, and speed with which the first spread, and other similar matters to be important indicators of a fire's cause. These are the kinds of things about which neighbors and other direct witnesses might have knowledge.
Def:	And what did you learn from those interviews in this case?
Fox:	Information supplied by these witnesses concerning the place where smoke first appeared, the color of the flames, and the speed of the fire's spread supported my view that the fire was of incendiary origin and that it began in the northeast corner of the first floor, where I found kerosene residue.
Def:	No further questions, Your Honor.

In this example, Defendant's counsel has successfully demonstrated the bases of the expert's opinion, primarily personal inspection and interviews of witnesses. In addition, counsel has shown that these sources are of a type reasonably relied upon by fire investigation experts.

PART 2:
COMPARISON OF FEDERAL RULES OF EVIDENCE AND CALIFORNIA EVIDENCE CODE

The following materials present a side-by-side comparison of the provisions of the Federal Rules of Evidence discussed in *Evidence: A Structured Approach* and their counterparts in the California Evidence Code. These codifications are similar in a great many areas, but there are also some important differences. To help you identify and understand the differences, we have included sets of "Questions for Classroom Discussion."

The materials are arranged in the order covered in the text, and can be studied when those sections of the book are discussed.

The following compilation arranges the Federal Rules and the California Evidence Code in adjoining vertical columns of text. Where there are provisions in both the Federal Rules and the California Evidence Code that address the same subject, those provisions usually appear side-by-side. Where a provision in one set of rules has no counterpart in the other set, the adjoining column will be blank. Sometimes the different length of comparable Federal and California provisions make it impossible to position them side-by-side, in which case they will at least appear on the same page.

Note that the California Evidence Code is considerably more detailed than the Federal Rules, and covers a number of areas not mentioned in the Federal Rules. The materials presented herein do not cover all sections of the California Evidence Code, but they do discuss all important differences between provisions of the Federal Rules and the California counterparts.

Students also need to be aware that California evidence law is affected in several important respects by the adoption of citizen initiatives over the last couple of decades. We do not attempt to canvas these initiatives here. However, certain key provisions of one such initiative are referenced in connection with impeachment of a witness's character, and the initiative is set forth more fully at the end of this book.

CHAPTER
1

The Process of Proof

B.   APPELLATE REVIEW OF EVIDENTIARY ISSUES

Fed. R. Evid. 103. Rulings on Evidence
(a) Effect of erroneous ruling.
Error may not be predicated upon a ruling which admits or excludes evidence unless a substantial right of the party is affected, and
(1) Objection. In case the ruling is one admitting evidence, a timely objection or motion to strike appears of record, stating the specific ground of objection, if the specific ground was not apparent from the context; or

(2) Offer of proof. In case the ruling is one excluding evidence, the substance of the evidence was made known to the court by offer or was apparent from the context within which questions were asked.

C.E.C. § 353. Erroneous admission of evidence; effect
A verdict or finding shall not be set aside, nor shall the judgment or decision based thereon be reversed, by reason of the erroneous admission of evidence unless:
(a) There appears of record an objection to or a motion to exclude or to strike the evidence that was timely made and so stated as to make clear the specific ground of the objection or motion; and
(b) The court which passes upon the effect of the error or errors is of the opinion that the admitted evidence should have been excluded on the ground stated and that the error or errors complained of resulted in a miscarriage of justice.

C.E.C. § 354. Erroneous exclusion of evidence; effect
A verdict or finding shall not be set aside, nor shall the judgment or decision based thereon be reversed, by reason of the erroneous exclusion of evidence unless the court which passes upon the effect of the error or errors is of the opinion that the error or errors complained of resulted in a miscarriage of justice and it appears of record that:
(a) The substance, purpose, and relevance of the excluded evidence was made known to the court by the questions asked, an offer of proof, or by any other means;

(b) The rulings of the court made compliance with subdivision (a) futile; or

(c) The evidence was sought by questions asked during cross-examination or recross-examination.

Once the court makes a definitive ruling on the record admitting or excluding evidence, either at or before trial, a party need not renew an objection or offer of proof to preserve a claim of error for appeal.

(b) Record of offer and ruling. The court may add any other or further statement which shows the character of the evidence, the form in which it was offered, the objection made, and the ruling thereon. It may direct the making of an offer in question and answer form.

(c) Hearing of jury. In jury cases, proceedings shall be conducted, to the extent practicable, so as to prevent inadmissible evidence from being suggested to the jury by any means, such as making statements or offers of proof or asking questions in the hearing of the jury.

(d) Plain error. Nothing in this rule precludes taking notice of plain errors affecting substantial rights although they were not brought to the attention of the court.

Questions for Classroom Discussion
Casebook page 24

1. Prosecution for Murder. The prosecution offers into evidence a letter from a witness to the crime. The defense objects on the ground of hearsay and the objection is sustained. The prosecution then offers a second letter from the same witness. The defense attorney objects, but fails to state a specific ground for the

objection. The court overrules the objection and admits the second letter. Has the defense waived the hearsay objection for purposes of appeal? What arguments may be made on the basis of the text of the federal and California provisions?

2. Same case. Before trial the court ruled both letters inadmissible. The defense failed to object at trial when the prosecution offered the letters into evidence and the trial court admitted them. Has the defense waived its objections for purposes of appeal? What arguments may be made on the basis of the text of the federal and California provisions?

3. Same case. The defense objects to both letters on the ground of hearsay. The trial judge states in open court and in the hearing of the jury, "objection sustained but it doesn't matter, since defendant is obviously guilty." If the defense fails to object to the judge's statement, has it waived the matter for purposes of appeal? What arguments may be made on the basis of the text of the federal and California provisions?

C.   SOURCES OF EVIDENCE AND THE NATURE OF PROOF

2.   *Witnesses: The Requirements of Competency, Personal Knowledge, and Oath or Affirmation*

a.   "Competent to Be a Witness"

Fed. R. Evid. 601. General Rule of Competency	C.E.C. § 700. General rule as to competency
Every person is competent to be a witness except as otherwise provided in these rules. However, in civil actions and proceedings, with respect to an element of a claim or defense as to which State law supplies the rule of decision, the competency of a witness shall be determined in accordance with State law.	Except as otherwise provided by statute, every person, irrespective of age, is qualified to be a witness and no person is disqualified to testify to any matter.

C.E.C. § 701. Disqualification of witness

(a) A person is disqualified to be a witness if he or she is:

(1) Incapable of expressing himself or herself concerning the matter so as to be understood, either directly or through interpretation by one who can understand him; or

(2) Incapable of understanding the duty of a witness to tell the truth.

(b) In any proceeding held outside the presence of a jury, the court may reserve challenges to the competency of a witness until the conclusion of the direct examination of that witness.

C.E.C. § 795. Testimony of hypnosis subject; admissibility; conditions

(a) The testimony of a witness is not inadmissible in a criminal proceeding by reason of the fact that the witness has previously undergone hypnosis for the purpose of recalling events which are the subject of the witness' testimony, if all of the following conditions are met:

(1) The testimony is limited to those matters which the witness recalled and related prior to the hypnosis.

(2) The substance of the prehypnotic memory was preserved in written, audiotape, or videotape form prior to the hypnosis.

(3) The hypnosis was conducted in accordance with all of the following procedures:

(A) A written record was made prior to hypnosis documenting the subject's description of the event, and information which was provided to the hypnotist concerning the subject matter of the hypnosis.

(B) The subject gave informed consent to the hypnosis.

(C) The hypnosis session, including the pre- and post-hypnosis interviews, was videotape recorded for subsequent review. (D) The hypnosis was performed by a licensed medical doctor, psychologist, licensed clinical social worker, or a licensed marriage and family therapist experienced in the use of hypnosis and independent of and not in the presence of law enforcement, the prosecution, or the defense.

(4) Prior to admission of the testimony, the court holds a hearing pursuant to Section 402 of the Evidence Code at which the proponent of the evidence proves by clear and convincing evidence that the hypnosis did not so affect the witness as to render the witness' prehypnosis recollection unreliable or to substantially impair the ability to cross-examine the witness concerning the witness' prehypnosis recollection. At the hearing, each side shall have the right to present expert testimony and to cross-examine witnesses.

(b) Nothing in this section shall be construed to limit the ability of a party to attack the credibility of a witness who has undergone hypnosis, or to limit other legal grounds to admit or exclude the testimony of that witness.

Question for Classroom Discussion
Casebook page 27

Action for personal injuries sustained in an automobile accident. The only surviving passenger in plaintiff's car is a mentally retarded adult with limited ability to speak. She is non-responsive when asked if she understands that she must tell the truth while testifying. Is the witness competent under the Federal Rules? Under California law?

b.   Competency of Judge and Jurors

Fed. R. Evid. 605. Competency of Judge as Witness	**C.E.C.§ 703. Judge as witness**
The judge presiding at the trial may not testify in that trial as a witness. No objection need be made in order to preserve the point.	(a) Before the judge presiding at the trial of an action may be called to testify in that trial as a witness, he shall, in proceedings held out of the presence and hearing of the jury, inform the parties of the information he has concerning any fact or matter about which he will be called to testify. (b) Against the objection of a party, the judge presiding at the trial of an action may not testify in that trial as a witness. Upon such objection, the judge shall declare a mistrial and order the action assigned for trial before another judge. (c) The calling of the judge presiding at a trial to testify in that trial as a witness shall be deemed a consent to the granting of a motion for mistrial, and an objection to such calling of a judge shall be deemed a motion for mistrial. (d) In the absence of objection by a party, the judge presiding at the trial of an action may testify in that trial as a witness. **C.E.C. § 703.5. Judges, arbitrators or mediators as witnesses; subsequent civil proceeding** No person presiding at any judicial or quasi-judicial proceeding, and no arbitrator or mediator, shall be competent to testify, in any subsequent civil proceeding, as to any statement, conduct, decision, or ruling, occurring at or in conjunction with the prior proceeding, except as to a statement or conduct that could (a) give rise to civil or criminal contempt, (b) constitute a crime, (c) be the subject of investigation by the State Bar or Commission on Judicial Performance, or (d) give rise to disqualification proceedings under paragraph (1) or (6) of subdivision (a) of Section 170.1 of the Code of Civil

	Procedure. However, this section does not apply to a mediator with regard to any mediation under Chapter 11 (commencing with Section 3160) of Part 2 of Division 8 of the Family Code.

Question for Classroom Discussion
Casebook page 29

Prosecution for assault of a witness in a prior case. The prosecution calls the judge in the instant proceeding to testify. The defense does not object. Is the witness competent under the Federal Rules? Under the C.E.C.?

Fed. R. Evid. 606. Competency of Juror as Witness	C.E.C. § 704. Juror as witness
(a) At the trial. A member of the jury may not testify as a witness before that jury in the trial of the case in which the juror is sitting. If the juror is called so to testify, the opposing party shall be afforded an opportunity to object out of the presence of the jury.	(a) Before a juror sworn and impaneled in the trial of an action may be called to testify before the jury in that trial as a witness, he shall, in proceedings conducted by the court out of the presence and hearing of the remaining jurors, inform the parties of the information he has concerning any fact or matter about which he will be called to testify.
	(b) Against the objection of a party, a juror sworn and impaneled in the trial of an action may not testify before the jury in that trial as a witness. Upon such objection, the court shall declare a mistrial and order the action assigned for trial before another jury.
	(c) The calling of a juror to testify before the jury as a witness shall be deemed a consent to the granting of a motion for mistrial, and an objection to such calling of a juror shall be deemed a motion for mistrial.
	(d) In the absence of objection by a party, a juror sworn and impaneled in the trial of an action may be compelled to testify in that trial as a witness.

(b) Inquiry into validity of verdict or indictment. Upon an inquiry into the validity of a verdict or indictment, a juror may not testify as to any matter or statement occurring during the course of the jury's deliberations or to the effect of anything upon that or any other juror's mind or emotions as influencing the juror to assent to or dissent from the verdict or indictment or concerning the juror's mental processes in connection therewith. But a juror may testify about (1) whether extraneous prejudicial information was improperly brought to the jury's attention, (2) whether any outside influence was improperly brought to bear upon any juror, or (3) whether there was a mistake in entering the verdict onto the verdict form. A juror's affidavit or evidence of any statement by the juror may not be received on a matter about which the juror would be precluded from testifying.

C.E.C. § 1150. Evidence to test a verdict
(a) Upon an inquiry as to the validity of a verdict, any otherwise admissible evidence may be received as to statements made, or conduct, conditions, or events occurring, either within or without the jury room, of such a character as is likely to have influenced the verdict improperly. No evidence is admissible to show the effect of such statement, conduct, condition, or event upon a juror either in influencing him to assent to or dissent from the verdict or concerning the mental processes by which it was determined.
(b) Nothing in this code affects the law relating to the competence of a juror to give evidence to impeach or support a verdict.

Questions for Classroom Discussion
Casebook page 32

1. Prosecution for bank robbery. The prosecutor calls a member of the jury to testify as to the layout of the bank, where the juror has a checking account. The defense does not object. Is the juror competent to testify under the Federal Rules? Under the C.E.C.?

2. Same case. Immediately after the prosecution puts the juror on the stand the judge calls for a recess. During the recess the defense objects to the juror testifying. How does this objection affect the trial under the Federal Rules? Under the C.E.C.?

3. Same case. After the jury returns a verdict of guilty, the defense makes a motion for a new trial. During the hearing on that motion, the defense offers the testimony of a member of the jury who offers to testify that, during deliberations, several members of the jury were drinking and intoxicated. Is the juror competent under the Federal Rules? Under the C.E.C.?

d. The "Personal Knowledge" Requirement

Fed. R. Evid. 602. Lack of Personal Knowledge	**C.E.C. § 702. Personal knowledge of witness**
A witness may not testify to a matter unless evidence is introduced sufficient to support a finding that the witness has personal knowledge of the matter. Evidence to prove personal knowledge may, but need not, consist of the witness' own testimony. This rule is subject to the provisions of Rule 703, relating to opinion testimony by expert witnesses.	(a) Subject to Section 801, the testimony of a witness concerning a particular matter is inadmissible unless he has personal knowledge of the matter. Against the objection of a party, such personal knowledge must be shown before the witness may testify concerning the matter. (b) A witness' personal knowledge of a matter may be shown by any otherwise admissible evidence, including his own testimony.
	C.E.C. § 403. Determination of foundational and other preliminary facts where relevancy, personal knowledge, or authenticity is disputed
	(a) The proponent of the proffered evidence has the burden of producing evidence as to the existence of the preliminary fact, and the proffered evidence is inadmissible unless the court finds that there is evidence sufficient to sustain a finding of the existence of the preliminary fact, when: ... (2) The preliminary fact is the personal knowledge of a witness concerning the subject matter of his testimony....

1. Personal injury action arising out of trip and fall in supermarket. The defense calls the store manager to testify. He says he saw the accident and offers to testify as to what happened. Previously, witnesses testified that the manager was in the stockroom when the accident occurred at the front of the store. May the manager testify under the Federal Rules? Under the C.E.C.?

e.   The "Oath or Affirmation" Requirement

Fed. R. Evid. 603. Oath or Affirmation	C.E.C. § 710. Oath required
Before testifying, every witness shall be required to declare that the witness will testify truthfully, by oath or affirmation administered in a form calculated to awaken the witness' conscience and impress the witness' mind with the duty to do so.	Every witness before testifying shall take an oath or make an affirmation or declaration in the form provided by law, except that a child under the age of 10 or a dependent person with a substantial cognitive impairment, in the court's discretion, may be required only to promise to tell the truth.

3.   *Real evidence: Authentication and the Best Evidence Rule*

b.   Authentication

Fed. R. Evid. 901. Requirement of Authentication or Identification	C.E.C. § 1400. Authentication
(a) General provision. The requirement of authentication or identification as a condition precedent to admissibility is satisfied by evidence sufficient to support a finding that the matter in question is what its proponent claims. (b) Illustrations. By way of illustration only, and not by way of limitation, the following are	Authentication of a writing means (a) the introduction of evidence sufficient to sustain a finding that it is the writing that the proponent of the evidence claims it is or (b) the establishment of such facts by any other means provided by law. **C.E.C. § 1410. Article not exclusive** Nothing in this article shall be construed to limit the means by which a writing may be authenticated or proved.

examples of authentication or identification conforming with the requirements of this rule:

(1) Testimony of witness with knowledge. Testimony that a matter is what it is claimed to be.

C.E.C. § 1413. Witness to the execution of a writing
A writing may be authenticated by anyone who saw the writing made or executed, including a subscribing witness.

(2) Nonexpert opinion on handwriting. Nonexpert opinion as to the genuineness of handwriting, based upon familiarity not acquired for purposes of the litigation.

C.E.C. § 1416. Proof of handwriting by person familiar therewith
A witness who is not otherwise qualified to testify as an expert may state his opinion whether a writing is in the handwriting of a supposed writer if the court finds that he has personal knowledge of the handwriting of the supposed writer. Such personal knowledge may be acquired from:
(a) Having seen the supposed writer write;
(b) Having seen a writing purporting to be in the handwriting of the supposed writer and upon which the supposed writer has acted or been charged;
(c) Having received letters in the due course of mail purporting to be from the supposed writer in response to letters duly addressed and mailed by him to the supposed writer; or
(d) Any other means of obtaining personal knowledge of the handwriting of the supposed writer.

C.E.C. § 1417. Comparison of handwriting by trier of fact
The genuineness of handwriting, or the lack thereof, may be proved by a comparison made by the trier of fact with handwriting (a) which the court finds was admitted or treated as genuine by the party against whom the evidence is offered or (b) otherwise proved to be genuine to the satisfaction of the court.

(3) Comparison by trier or expert witness. Comparison by the trier of fact or by expert witnesses with specimens which have been authenticated.

	C.E.C. § 1418. Comparison of writing by expert witness The genuineness of writing, or the lack thereof, may be proved by a comparison made by an expert witness with writing (a) which the court finds was admitted or treated as genuine by the party against whom the evidence is offered or (b) otherwise proved to be genuine to the satisfaction of the court.
	C.E.C. § 1419. Exemplars when writing is more than 30 years old Where a writing whose genuineness is sought to be proved is more than 30 years old, the comparison under Section 1417 or 1418 may be made with writing purporting to be genuine, and generally respected and acted upon as such, by persons having an interest in knowing whether it is genuine.
(4) Distinctive characteristics and the like. Appearance, contents, substance, internal patterns, or other distinctive characteristics, taken in conjunction with circumstances.	
	C.E.C. § 1420. Authentication by evidence of reply A writing may be authenticated by evidence that the writing was received in response to a communication sent to the person who is claimed by the proponent of the evidence to be the author of the writing.
	C.E.C. § 1421. Authentication by content A writing may be authenticated by evidence that the writing refers to or states matters that are unlikely to be known to anyone other than the person who is claimed by the proponent of the evidence to be the author of the writing.

(5) Voice identification. Identification of a voice, whether heard firsthand or through mechanical or electronic transmission or recording, by opinion based upon hearing the voice at any time under circumstances connecting it with the alleged speaker.

(6) Telephone conversations. Telephone conversations, by evidence that a call was made to the number assigned at the time by the telephone company to a particular person or business, if (A) in the case of a person, circumstances, including self-identification, show the person answering to be the one called, or (B) in the case of a business, the call was made to a place of business and the conversation related to business reasonably transacted over the telephone.

(7) Public records or reports. Evidence that a writing authorized by law to be recorded or filed and in fact recorded or filed in a public office, or a purported public record, report, statement, or data compilation, in any form, is from the public office where items of this nature are kept.

C.E.C. § 1532. Official record of recorded writing
(a) The official record of a writing is prima facie evidence of the existence and content of the original recorded writing if:
(1) The record is in fact a record of an office of a public entity; and
(2) A statute authorized such a writing to be recorded in that office.
(b) The presumption established by this section is a presumption affecting the burden of producing evidence.

C.E.C. § 1600. Record of document affecting property interest
(a) The record of an instrument or other document purporting to establish or affect an interest in property is prima facie evidence of the existence and content of the original recorded document and its execution and delivery by each person by

(8) Ancient documents or data compilation. Evidence that a document or data compilation, in any form, (A) is in such condition as to create no suspicion concerning its authenticity, (B) was in a place where it, if authentic, would likely be, and (C) has been in existence 20 years or more at the time it is offered.

(9) Process or system. Evidence describing a process or system used to produce a result and showing that the process or system produces an accurate result.
(10) Methods provided by statute or rule. Any method of authentication or identification provided by Act of Congress or by other rules prescribed by the Supreme Court pursuant to statutory authority.

whom it purports to have been executed if:
(1) The record is in fact a record of an office of a public entity; and
(2) A statute authorized such a document to be recorded in that office.
(b) The presumption established by this section is a presumption affecting the burden of proof.

C.E.C. § 643. Authenticity of ancient document
A deed or will or other writing purporting to create, terminate, or affect an interest in real or personal property is presumed to be authentic if it:
(a) Is at least 30 years old;
(b) Is in such condition as to create no suspicion concerning its authenticity;
(c) Was kept, or if found was found, in a place where such writing, if authentic, would be likely to be kept or found; and
(d) Has been generally acted upon as authentic by persons having an interest in the matter.

1. Action for breach of contract. Plaintiff testifies that Exhibit A is the original contract. Defendant will testify to the contrary. Has Plaintiff offered sufficient evidence to authenticate Exhibit A under the Federal Rules? Under the C.E.C.?

2. Note that under the C.E.C., all provisions relating to authentication concern some form of a writing, broadly defined, while the scope of Rule 901 seems to be wider, applying to telephone conversations, voice identification, and the like. Is the authentication requirement under the C.E.C. limited to writings?

v. *Self-Authentication*

Fed. R. Evid. 902. Self-authentication Extrinsic evidence of authenticity as a condition precedent to admissibility is not required with respect to the following: (1) Domestic public documents under seal. A document bearing a seal purporting to be that of the United States, or of any State, district, Commonwealth, territory, or insular possession thereof, or the Panama Canal Zone, or the Trust Territory of the Pacific Islands, or of a political subdivision, department, officer, or agency thereof, and a signature purporting to be an attestation or execution.	**C.E.C. § 1452. Official seals** A seal is presumed to be genuine and its use authorized if it purports to be the seal of: (a) The United States or a department, agency, or public employee of the United States. (b) A public entity in the United States or a department, agency, or public employee of such public entity. (c) A nation recognized by the executive power of the United States or a department, agency, or officer of such nation. (d) A public entity in a nation recognized by the executive power of the United States or a department, agency, or officer of such public entity. (e) A court of admiralty or maritime jurisdiction. (f) A notary public within any state of the United States.

(2) Domestic public documents not under seal. A document purporting to bear the signature in the official capacity of an officer or employee of any entity included in paragraph (1) hereof, having no seal, if a public officer having a seal and having official duties in the district or political subdivision of the officer or employee certifies under seal that the signer has the official capacity and that the signature is genuine.

(3) Foreign public documents. A document purporting to be executed or attested in an official capacity by a person authorized by the laws of a foreign country to make the execution or attestation, and accompanied by a final certification as to the genuineness of the signature and official position (A) of the executing or attesting person, or (B) of any foreign official whose certificate of genuineness of signature and official position relates to the execution or attestation or is in a chain of certificates of genuineness of signature and official position relating to the execution or attestation. A final certification may be made by a secretary of an embassy or legation, consul general, consul, vice consul, or consular agent of the United States, or a diplomatic or consular official of the foreign country assigned or accredited to the United States. If reasonable opportunity has been given to all parties to investigate the authenticity and accuracy of official documents, the court may, for good cause shown, order that they be treated as presumptively authentic

C.E.C. § 1453. Domestic official signatures

A signature is presumed to be genuine and authorized if it purports to be the signature, affixed in his official capacity, of:
(a) A public employee of the United States.
(b) A public employee of any public entity in the United States.
(c) A notary public within any state of the United States.

C.E.C. § 1454. Foreign official signatures

A signature is presumed to be genuine and authorized if it purports to be the signature, affixed in his official capacity, of an officer, or deputy of an officer, of a nation or public entity in a nation recognized by the executive power of the United States and the writing to which the signature is affixed is accompanied by a final statement certifying the genuineness of the signature and the official position of (a) the person who executed the writing or (b) any foreign official who has certified either the genuineness of the signature and official position of the person executing the writing or the genuineness of the signature and official position of another foreign official who has executed a similar certificate in a chain of such certificates beginning with a certificate of the genuineness of the signature and official position of the person executing the writing. The final statement may be made only by a secretary of an embassy or legation, consul general, consul, vice consul, consular agent, or other officer in the foreign service of the United States stationed in the nation, authenticated by the seal of his office.

without final certification or permit them to be evidenced by an attested summary with or without final certification.

(4) Certified copies of public records. A copy of an official record or report or entry therein, or of a document authorized by law to be recorded or filed and actually recorded or filed in a public office, including data compilations in any form, certified as correct by the custodian or other person authorized to make the certification, by certificate complying with paragraph (1), (2), or (3) of this rule or complying with any Act of Congress or rule prescribed by the Supreme Court pursuant to statutory authority.

C.E.C. § 1530. Copy of writing in official custody

(a) A purported copy of a writing in the custody of a public entity, or of an entry in such a writing, is prima facie evidence of the existence and content of such writing or entry if:

(1) The copy purports to be published by the authority of the nation or state, or public entity therein in which the writing is kept;

(2) The office in which the writing is kept is within the United States or within the Panama Canal Zone, the Trust Territory of the Pacific Islands, or the Ryukyu Islands, and the copy is attested or certified as a correct copy of the writing or entry by a public employee, or a deputy of a public employee, having the legal custody of the writing; or

(3) The office in which the writing is kept is not within the United States or any other place described in paragraph (2) and the copy is attested as a correct copy of the writing or entry by a person having authority to make attestation. The attestation must be accompanied by a final statement certifying the genuineness of the signature and the official position of (i) the person who attested the copy as a correct copy or (ii) any foreign official who has certified either the genuineness of the signature and official position of the person attesting the copy or the genuineness of the signature and official position of another foreign official who has executed a similar certificate in a chain of such certificates beginning with a certificate of the genuineness of the signature and official position of the person attesting the copy. Except as provided in the next sentence, the final statement may be made only by a

	secretary of an embassy or legation, consul general, consul, vice consul, or consular agent of the United States, or a diplomatic or consular official of the foreign country assigned or accredited to the United States. Prior to January 1, 1971, the final statement may also be made by a secretary of an embassy or legation, consul general, consul, vice consul, consular agent, or other officer in the foreign service of the United States stationed in the nation in which the writing is kept, authenticated by the seal of his office. If reasonable opportunity has been given to all parties to investigate the authenticity and accuracy of the documents, the court may, for good cause shown, (i) admit an attested copy without the final statement or (ii) permit the writing or entry in foreign custody to be evidenced by an attested summary with or without a final statement.
(5) Official publications. Books, pamphlets, or other publications purporting to be issued by public authority.	**C.E.C. § 644. Book purporting to be published by public authority** A book, purporting to be printed or published by public authority, is presumed to have been so printed or published. **C.E.C. § 645. Book purporting to contain reports of cases** A book, purporting to contain reports of cases adjudged in the tribunals of the state or nation where the book is published, is presumed to contain correct reports of such cases.
(6) Newspapers and periodicals. Printed materials purporting to be newspapers or periodicals.	**C.E.C. § 645.1. Printed materials purporting to be particular newspaper or periodical** Printed materials, purporting to be a particular newspaper or periodical, are presumed to be that newspaper or periodical if regularly issued at average intervals not exceeding three months.

(7) Trade inscriptions and the like. Inscriptions, signs, tags, or labels purporting to have been affixed in the course of business and indicating ownership, control, or origin.

(8) Acknowledged documents. Documents accompanied by a certificate of acknowledgment executed in the manner provided by law by a notary public or other officer authorized by law to take acknowledgments.

C.E.C. § 1451. Acknowledged writings
A certificate of the acknowledgment of a writing other than a will, or a certificate of the proof of such a writing, is prima facie evidence of the facts recited in the certificate and the genuineness of the signature of each person by whom the writing purports to have been signed if the certificate meets the requirements of Article 3 (commencing with Section 1180) of Chapter 4, Title 4, Part 4, Division 2 of the Civil Code.

(9) Commercial paper and related documents. Commercial paper, signatures thereon, and documents relating thereto to the extent provided by general commercial law.
(10) Presumptions under Acts of Congress. Any signature, document, or other matter declared by Act of Congress to be presumptively or prima facie genuine or authentic.
(11) Certified Domestic Records of Regularly Conducted Activity.--The original or a duplicate of a domestic record of regularly conducted activity that would be admissible under Rule 803(6) if accompanied by a written declaration of its custodian or other qualified person, in a manner complying with any Act of Congress or rule prescribed by the Supreme Court pursuant to statutory authority, certifying that the record—

(A) was made at or near the time of the occurrence of the matters set forth by, or from information transmitted by, a person with knowledge of those matters;
(B) was kept in the course of the regularly conducted activity; and
(C) was made by the regularly conducted activity as a regular practice.
A party intending to offer a record into evidence under this paragraph must provide written notice of that intention to all adverse parties, and must make the record and declaration available for inspection sufficiently in advance of their offer into evidence to provide an adverse party with a fair opportunity to challenge them.
(12) Certified Foreign Records of Regularly Conducted Activity.—In a civil case, the original or a duplicate of a foreign record of regularly conducted activity that would be admissible under Rule 803(6) if accompanied by a written declaration by its custodian or other qualified person certifying that the record—
(A) was made at or near the time of the occurrence of the matters set forth by, or from information transmitted by, a person with knowledge of those matters;
(B) was kept in the course of the regularly conducted activity; and
(C) was made by the regularly conducted activity as a regular practice.
The declaration must be signed in a manner that, if falsely made, would subject the maker to criminal penalty under the laws of the country where the declaration is signed. A party intending to offer a

record into evidence under this paragraph must provide written notice of that intention to all adverse parties, and must make the record and declaration available for inspection sufficiently in advance of their offer into evidence to provide an adverse party with a fair opportunity to challenge them.	

Questions for Classroom Discussion
Casebook page 61

1. Personal injury action. Plaintiff alleges that he was drinking a bottle of Whoopsi Cola when he discovered a human finger in the bottle. Defendant denies it was a bottle of Whoopsi Cola. Plaintiff offers Exhibit A, a bottle imprinted with the words "Whoopsi Cola" on the side and he testifies it is the bottle from which he was drinking. Is the imprint on the bottle sufficient under the Federal Rules and the C.E.C. to authenticate the exhibit as a bottle manufactured by Defendant or is additional evidence necessary?

2. Civil action for violation of antitrust laws. Defendant offers into evidence hundreds of documents from its internal business files to prove it was not fixing prices. Under the Federal Rules, is it necessary for defendant to call a witness to authenticate each document or is there a quicker way? How about under the C.E.C.?

c.   **The Best Evidence Rule**

i.   *The Basic Rule*

Fed. R. Evid. 1001. Definitions	
For purposes of this article the following definitions are applicable:	
(1) Writings and recordings. "Writings" and "recordings" consist of letters, words, or numbers, or their equivalent, set down by handwriting, typewriting, printing, photostating, photographing, magnetic	**C.E.C. § 250. Writing** "Writing" means handwriting, typewriting, printing, photostating, photographing, photocopying, transmitting by electronic mail or facsimile, and every other means of

impulse, mechanical or electronic recording, or other form of data compilation.

(2) Photographs. "Photographs" include still photographs, X-ray films, video tapes, and motion pictures.

(3) Original. An "original" of a writing or recording is the writing or recording itself or any counterpart intended to have the same effect by a person executing or issuing it. An "original" of a photograph includes the negative or any print therefrom. If data are stored in a computer or similar device, any printout or other output readable by sight, shown to reflect the data accurately, is an "original".

(4) Duplicate. A "duplicate" is a counterpart produced by the same impression as the original, or from the same matrix, or by means of photography, including enlargements and miniatures, or by mechanical or electronic re-recording, or by chemical reproduction, or by other equivalent techniques which accurately reproduces the original.

recording upon any tangible thing, any form of communication or representation, including letters, words, pictures, sounds, or symbols, or combinations thereof, and any record thereby created, regardless of the manner in which the record has been stored.

C.E.C. § 255. Original
"Original" means the writing itself or any counterpart intended to have the same effect by a person executing or issuing it. An "original" of a photograph includes the negative or any print therefrom. If data are stored in a computer or similar device, any printout or other output readable by sight, shown to reflect the data accurately, is an "original."

C.E.C. § 260. Duplicate
A "duplicate" is a counterpart produced by the same impression as the original, or from the same matrix, or by means of photography, including enlargements and miniatures, or by mechanical or electronic rerecording, or by chemical reproduction, or by other equivalent technique which accurately reproduces the original.

Fed. R. Evid. 1002. Requirement of Original
To prove the content of a writing, recording, or photograph, the original writing, recording, or photograph is required, except as otherwise provided in these rules or by Act of Congress.

C.E.C. § 1520. Content of writing; proof
The content of a writing may be proved by an otherwise admissible original.

Fed. R. Evid. 1003. Admissibility of Duplicates

A duplicate is admissible to the same extent as an original unless (1) a genuine question is raised as to the authenticity of the original or (2) in the circumstances it would be unfair to admit the duplicate in lieu of the original.

Fed. R. Evid. 1004. Admissibility of Other Evidence of Contents

The original is not required, and other evidence of the contents of a writing, recording, or photograph is admissible if—

(1) Originals lost or destroyed. All originals are lost or have been destroyed, unless the proponent lost or destroyed them in bad faith; or

(2) Original not obtainable. No original can be obtained by any available judicial process or procedure; or

(3) Original in possession of opponent. At a time when an original was under the control of the party against whom offered, that party was put on notice, by the pleadings or otherwise, that the contents would be a subject of proof at the hearing, and that party does not produce the original at the hearing; or

(4) Collateral matters. The writing, recording, or photograph is not closely related to a controlling issue.

C.E.C. § 1521. Secondary evidence rule

(a) The content of a writing may be proved by otherwise admissible secondary evidence. The court shall exclude secondary evidence of the content of writing if the court determines either of the following:

(1) A genuine dispute exists concerning material terms of the writing and justice requires the exclusion.

(2) Admission of the secondary evidence would be unfair.

(b) Nothing in this section makes admissible oral testimony to prove the content of a writing if the testimony is inadmissible under Section 1523 (oral testimony of the content of a writing).

(c) Nothing in this section excuses compliance with Section 1401 (authentication).

(d) This section shall be known as the "Secondary Evidence Rule."

C.E.C. § 1522. Additional grounds for exclusion of secondary evidence

(a) In addition to the grounds for exclusion authorized by Section 1521, in a criminal action the court shall exclude secondary evidence of the content of a writing if the court determines that the original is in the proponent's possession, custody, or control, and the proponent has not made the original reasonably available for inspection at or before trial. This section does not apply to any of the following:

(1) A duplicate as defined in Section 260.

(2) A writing that is not closely related to the controlling issues in the action.

(3) A copy of a writing in the custody of a public entity.

(4) A copy of a writing that is recorded in the public records, if the record or a certified copy of it is made evidence of the

writing by statute.

(b) In a criminal action, a request to exclude secondary evidence of the content of a writing, under this section or any other law, shall not be made in the presence of the jury.

C.E.C. § 1523. Oral testimony of the content of a writing; admissibility
(a) Except as otherwise provided by statute, oral testimony is not admissible to prove the content of a writing.
(b) Oral testimony of the content of a writing is not made inadmissible by subdivision (a) if the proponent does not have possession or control of a copy of the writing and the original is lost or has been destroyed without fraudulent intent on the part of the proponent of the evidence.
(c) Oral testimony of the content of a writing is not made inadmissible by subdivision (a) if the proponent does not have possession or control of the original or a copy of the writing and either of the following conditions is satisfied:
(1) Neither the writing nor a copy of the writing was reasonably procurable by the proponent by use of the court's process or by other available means.
(2) The writing is not closely related to the controlling issues and it would be inexpedient to require its production.
(d) Oral testimony of the content of a writing is not made inadmissible by subdivision (a) if the writing consists of numerous accounts or other writings that cannot be examined in court without great loss of time, and the evidence sought from them is only the general result of the whole.

Fed. R. Evid. 1006. Summaries
The contents of voluminous writings, recordings, or photographs which cannot conveniently be examined in court may be presented in the form of a chart, summary, or calculation. The originals, or duplicates, shall be made available for examination or copying, or both, by other parties at reasonable time and place. The court may order that they be produced in court.

C.E.C. § 1550. Photographic copies made as business records

(a) If made and preserved as a part of the records of a business, as defined in Section 1270, in the regular course of that business, the following types of evidence of a writing are as admissible as the writing itself:

(1) A nonerasable optical image reproduction or any other reproduction of a public record by a trusted system, as defined in Section 12168.7 of the Government Code, if additions, deletions, or changes to the original document are not permitted by the technology.

(2) A photostatic copy or reproduction.

(3) A microfilm, microcard, or miniature photographic copy, reprint, or enlargement.

(4) Any other photographic copy or reproduction, or an enlargement thereof.

(b) The introduction of evidence of a writing pursuant to subdivision (a) does not preclude admission of the original writing if it is still in existence. A court may require the introduction of a hard copy printout of the document.

C.E.C. § 1550.1. Admissibility of reproductions of files, records, writings, photographs, and fingerprints

Reproductions of files, records, writings, photographs, fingerprints or other instruments in the official custody of a criminal justice agency that were microphotographed or otherwise reproduced in a manner that conforms with the provisions of Section 11106.1, 11106.2, or 11106.3 of the Penal Code shall be admissible to the same extent and under the same circumstances as the original file, record, writing or other instrument would be admissible.

C.E.C. § 1551. Photographic copies where original destroyed or lost
A print, whether enlarged or not, from a photographic film (including a photographic plate, microphotographic film, photostatic negative, or similar reproduction) of an original writing destroyed or lost after such film was taken or a reproduction from an electronic recording of video images on magnetic surfaces is admissible as the original writing itself if, at the time of the taking of such film or electronic recording, the person under whose direction and control it was taken attached thereto, or to the sealed container in which it was placed and has been kept, or incorporated in the film or electronic recording, a certification complying with the provisions of Section 1531 and stating the date on which, and the fact that, it was so taken under his direction and control.

C.E.C. § 1552. Printed representation of computer information or computer programs
(a) A printed representation of computer information or a computer program is presumed to be an accurate representation of the computer information or computer program that it purports to represent. This presumption is a presumption affecting the burden of producing evidence. If a party to an action introduces evidence that a printed representation of computer information or computer program is inaccurate or unreliable, the party introducing the printed representation into evidence has the burden of proving, by a preponderance of evidence, that the printed representation is an accurate representation of the existence and content of the computer information or computer program that it purports to represent.
(b) Subdivision (a) shall not apply to

computer-generated official records certified in accordance with Section 452.5 or 1530.

C.E.C. § 1553. Printed representation of images stored on a video or digital medium

A printed representation of images stored on a video or digital medium is presumed to be an accurate representation of the images it purports to represent. This presumption is a presumption affecting the burden of producing evidence. If a party to an action introduces evidence that a printed representation of images stored on a video or digital medium is inaccurate or unreliable, the party introducing the printed representation into evidence has the burden of proving, by a preponderance of evidence, that the printed representation is an accurate representation of the existence and content of the images that it purports to represent.

Questions for Classroom Discussion
Casebook page 66

1. Civil action for breach of a written contract alleging Defendant breached because it performed late. Plaintiff offers into evidence a photocopy of the contract to prove that Defendant's performance was due on September 1. The evidence will show that Plaintiff destroyed the original in order to conceal the fact that the word "November" had been typed over to appear to read "September." Is the photocopy admissible as a "duplicate" under Federal Rule 1003? If not, how would you phrase the objection if the evidence was then offered under Rule 1002? Is the photocopy admissible under either C.E.C. § 1520 or 1521? If not, would you phrase the objection differently?

2. Same case. The contract was in the form of emails exchanged between Plaintiff and Defendant. The emails were saved to the hard disk in Plaintiff's laptop computer. Plaintiff offers into evidence printed copies of the emails produced by connecting a printer to his laptop. Are the copies admissible under the Federal Rules? Under the C.E.C.?

3. Civil action for trespass. Plaintiff offers a certified copy of his deed, obtained from the county recorder's office, to show the boundaries of his property. How will Plaintiff establish the authenticity of the document under California law? How will she meet the requirements of California's "Secondary Evidence Rule"? Could Plaintiff overcome authenticity and best evidence rule objections under the Federal Rules?

4. *Judicial Notice*

	C.E.C. § 450. Judicial notice may be taken only as authorized by law
	Judicial notice may not be taken of any matter unless authorized or required by law.
Fed. R. Evid. 201. Judicial Notice of Adjudicative Facts	**C.E.C. § 451. Matters which must be judicially noticed**
(a) Scope of rule. This rule governs only judicial notice of adjudicative facts.	Judicial notice shall be taken of the following:
(b) Kinds of facts. A judicially noticed fact must be one not subject to reasonable dispute in that it is either (1) generally known within the territorial jurisdiction of the trial court or (2) capable of accurate and ready determination by resort to sources whose accuracy cannot reasonably be questioned.	(a) The decisional, constitutional, and public statutory law of this state and of the United States and the provisions of any charter described in Section 3, 4, or 5 of Article XI of the California Constitution.
	(b) Any matter made a subject of judicial notice by Section 11343.6, 11344.6, or 18576 of the Government Code or by Section 1507 of Title 44 of the United States Code.
	(c) Rules of professional conduct for members of the bar adopted pursuant to Section 6076 of the Business and Professions Code and rules of practice and procedure for the courts of this state adopted by the Judicial Council.
	(d) Rules of pleading, practice, and procedure prescribed by the United States Supreme Court, such as the Rules of the United States Supreme Court, the Federal Rules of Civil Procedure, the Federal Rules of Criminal Procedure, the Admiralty Rules, the Rules of the Court of Claims, the Rules of the Customs Court, and the General Orders and Forms in Bankruptcy.

(e) The true signification of all English words and phrases and of all legal expressions.

(f) Facts and propositions of generalized knowledge that are so universally known that they cannot reasonably be the subject of dispute.

C.E.C. § 452. Matters which may be judicially noticed

Judicial notice may be taken of the following matters to the extent that they are not embraced within Section 451:

(a) The decisional, constitutional, and statutory law of any state of the United States and the resolutions and private acts of the Congress of the United States and of the Legislature of this state.

(b) Regulations and legislative enactments issued by or under the authority of the United States or any public entity in the United States.

(c) Official acts of the legislative, executive, and judicial departments of the United States and of any state of the United States.

(d) Records of (1) any court of this state or (2) any court of record of the United States or of any state of the United States.

(e) Rules of court of (1) any court of this state or (2) any court of record of the United States or of any state of the United States.

(f) The law of an organization of nations and of foreign nations and public entities in foreign nations.

(g) Facts and propositions that are of such common knowledge within the territorial jurisdiction of the court that they cannot reasonably be the subject of dispute.

(h) Facts and propositions that are not reasonably subject to dispute and are capable of immediate and accurate determination by resort to sources of reasonably indisputable accuracy.

(c) When discretionary. A court may take judicial notice, whether requested or not.

C.E.C. § 452.5. Criminal conviction records; computer-generated records; admissibility

(a) The official acts and records specified in subdivisions (c) and (d) of Section 452 include any computer-generated official court records, as specified by the Judicial Council which relate to criminal convictions, when the record is certified by a clerk of the superior court pursuant to Section 69844.5 of the Government Code at the time of computer entry.

(b) An official record of conviction certified in accordance with subdivision (a) of Section 1530 is admissible pursuant to Section 1280 to prove the commission, attempted commission, or solicitation of a criminal offense, prior conviction, service of a prison term, or other act, condition, or event recorded by the record.

(d) When mandatory. A court shall take judicial notice if requested by a party and supplied with the necessary information.

C.E.C. § 453. Compulsory judicial notice upon request

The trial court shall take judicial notice of any matter specified in Section 452 if a party requests it and:

(a) Gives each adverse party sufficient notice of the request, through the pleadings or otherwise, to enable such adverse party to prepare to meet the request; and

(b) Furnishes the court with sufficient information to enable it to take judicial notice of the matter.

§ 454. Information that may be used in taking judicial notice

(a) In determining the propriety of taking judicial notice of a matter, or the tenor thereof:

(1) Any source of pertinent information, including the advice of persons learned in the subject matter, may be consulted or used, whether or not furnished by a party.

(2) Exclusionary rules of evidence do not

apply except for Section 352 and the rules of privilege.

(b) Where the subject of judicial notice is the law of an organization of nations, a foreign nation, or a public entity in a foreign nation and the court resorts to the advice of persons learned in the subject matter, such advice, if not received in open court, shall be in writing.

C.E.C. § 455. Opportunity to present information to court

With respect to any matter specified in Section 452 or in subdivision (f) of Section 451 that is of substantial consequence to the determination of the action:

(a) If the trial court has been requested to take or has taken or proposes to take judicial notice of such matter, the court shall afford each party reasonable opportunity, before the jury is instructed or before the cause is submitted for decision by the court, to present to the court information relevant to (1) the propriety of taking judicial notice of the matter and (2) the tenor of the matter to be noticed.

(b) If the trial court resorts to any source of information not received in open court, including the advice of persons learned in the subject matter, such information and its source shall be made a part of the record in the action and the court shall afford each party reasonable opportunity to meet such information before judicial notice of the matter may be taken.

(e) Opportunity to be heard. A party is entitled upon timely request to an opportunity to be heard as to the propriety of taking judicial notice and the tenor of the matter noticed. In the absence of prior notification, the request may be made after judicial notice has been taken.

C.E.C. § 458. Judicial notice by trial court in subsequent proceedings

The failure or refusal of the trial court to take judicial notice of a matter, or to instruct the jury with respect to the matter, does not preclude the trial court in subsequent proceedings in the action from taking judicial notice of the matter in accordance with the procedure specified in this division.

(f) Time of taking notice. Judicial notice may be taken at any stage of the proceeding.

C.E.C. § 459. Judicial notice by reviewing court

(a) The reviewing court shall take judicial notice of (1) each matter properly noticed by the trial court and (2) each matter that the trial court was required to notice under Section 451 or 453. The reviewing court may take judicial notice of any matter specified in Section 452. The reviewing court may take judicial notice of a matter in a tenor different from that noticed by the trial court.

(b) In determining the propriety of taking judicial notice of a matter, or the tenor thereof, the reviewing court has the same power as the trial court under Section 454.

(c) When taking judicial notice under this section of a matter specified in Section 452 or in subdivision (f) of Section 451 that is of substantial consequence to the determination of the action, the reviewing court shall comply with the provisions of subdivision (a) of Section 455 if the matter was not theretofore judicially noticed in the action.

(d) In determining the propriety of taking judicial notice of a matter specified in Section 452 or in subdivision (f) of Section 451 that is of substantial consequence to the determination of the action, or the tenor thereof, if the reviewing court resorts to any source of information not received in open court or not included in the record of the action, including the advice of persons learned in the subject matter, the reviewing court shall afford each party reasonable opportunity to meet such information before judicial notice of the matter may be taken.

C.E.C. § 457. Instructing jury on matter judicially noticed

If a matter judicially noticed is a matter which would otherwise have been for determination by the jury, the trial court

(g) Instructing jury. In a civil action or proceeding, the court shall instruct the jury to accept as conclusive any fact judicially

| noticed. In a criminal case, the court shall instruct the jury that it may, but is not required to, accept as conclusive any fact judicially noticed. | may, and upon request shall, instruct the jury to accept as a fact the matter so noticed. |

Questions for Classroom Discussion
Casebook page 75

Prosecution for manslaughter arising out of an automobile accident. Defendant testifies that, as he was proceeding westbound on Main Street at 7 a.m., the sun was in his eyes and momentarily blinded him. Both sides rest their respective cases without offering any evidence as to the position of the sun at 7 a.m. on the date in question and neither side asked the court to take judicial notice thereof. The trial judge now wants to take judicial notice of the fact that the sun rises in the east and intends to instruct the jury accordingly. Answer each of the following questions under both the Federal Rules and the California Evidence Code:

1. Is the fact that the sun rises in the east subject to judicial notice?

2. Assuming this is a proper matter for judicial notice, is the court required to take judicial notice of this fact or is it a matter within the court's discretion?

3. Assuming the court properly takes judicial notice of this fact after requested to do so by the prosecution, should it instruct the jury that it must or may accept as fact that the sun rises in the east?

CHAPTER 2

Relevance

Fed. R. Evid. 401. Definition of "Relevant Evidence"
"Relevant evidence" means evidence having any tendency to make the existence of any fact that is of consequence to the determination of the action more probable or less probable than it would be without the evidence.

Fed. R. Evid. 402. Relevant Evidence Generally Admissible; Irrelevant Evidence Inadmissible
All relevant evidence is admissible, except as otherwise provided by the Constitution of the United States, by Act of Congress, by these rules, or by other rules prescribed by the Supreme Court pursuant to statutory authority. Evidence which is not relevant is not admissible.

C.E.C. § 210. Relevant evidence
"Relevant evidence" means evidence, including evidence relevant to the credibility of a witness or hearsay declarant, having any tendency in reason to prove or disprove any disputed fact that is of consequence to the determination of the action.

C.E.C. § 351. Admissibility of relevant evidence
Except as otherwise provided by statute, all relevant evidence is admissible.

Cal. Const. Art. I, § 28(d). Right to Truth-in-Evidence
Except as provided by statute hereafter enacted by a two-thirds vote of the membership in each house of the Legislature, relevant evidence shall not be excluded in any criminal proceeding, including pretrial and post conviction motions and hearings, or in any trial or hearing of a juvenile for a criminal offense, whether heard in juvenile or adult court. Nothing in this section shall affect any existing statutory rule of evidence relating to privilege or hearsay, or Evidence Code, Sections 352, 782 or 1103. Nothing in this section shall affect any existing statutory or constitutional right of the press.

B. BALANCING PROBATIVE VALUE AGAINST DANGERS

Fed. R. Evid. 403. Exclusion of Relevant Evidence on Grounds of Prejudice, Confusion, or Waste of Time	C.E.C. § 352. Discretion of court to exclude evidence
Although relevant, evidence may be excluded if its probative value is substantially outweighed by the danger of unfair prejudice, confusion of the issues, or misleading the jury, or by considerations of undue delay, waste of time, or needless presentation of cumulative evidence.	The court in its discretion may exclude evidence if its probative value is substantially outweighed by the probability that its admission will (a) necessitate undue consumption of time or (b) create substantial danger of undue prejudice, of confusing the issues, or of misleading the jury.

Questions for Classroom Discussion
Casebook page 97

1. Prosecution for being a felon in possession of a firearm. Defendant offered to stipulate that he has a felony conviction on his record but denied being in possession of a firearm. The prosecution accepted the stipulation and the court permitted the stipulation to be read to the jury. At trial the prosecution offered into evidence a certified copy of Defendant's judgment of conviction for carrying a firearm onto an airplane, which is a felony. Is this evidence relevant under the Federal Rules? The California Evidence Code? If relevant, what other objection might the defense raise?

2. Same case. Assume that under California evidence law covered later in the course, evidence that the defendant illegally possessed guns on some prior occasion is not admissible to show he has the *propensity* to act in that way and, thus, probably was in possession of a firearm on the occasion in question. Notwithstanding those rules, does Article I § 28(d) of the California Constitution make that evidence admissible? Notwithstanding that provision, can you object to the admission of that evidence under some other provision in the C.E.C.?

E. A SPECIAL APPLICATION OF RELEVANCE DOCTRINE: PRELIMINARY QUESTIONS OF FACT

Fed. R. Evid. 104. Preliminary Questions

(a) Questions of admissibility generally. Preliminary questions concerning the qualification of a person to be a witness, the existence of a privilege, or the admissibility of evidence shall be determined by the court, subject to the provisions of subdivision (b). In making its determination it is not bound by the rules of evidence except those with respect to privileges.

C.E.C. § 400. Preliminary fact

As used in this article, "preliminary fact" means a fact upon the existence or nonexistence of which depends the admissibility or inadmissibility of evidence. The phrase "the admissibility or inadmissibility of evidence" includes the qualification or disqualification of a person to be a witness and the existence or nonexistence of a privilege.

C.E.C. § 401. Proffered evidence

As used in this article, "proffered evidence" means evidence, the admissibility or inadmissibility of which is dependent upon the existence or nonexistence of a preliminary fact.

C.E.C. § 405. Determination of foundational and other preliminary facts in other cases

With respect to preliminary fact determinations not governed by Section 403 or 404:

(a) When the existence of a preliminary fact is disputed, the court shall indicate which party has the burden of producing evidence and the burden of proof on the issue as implied by the rule of law under which the question arises. The court shall determine the existence or nonexistence of the preliminary fact and shall admit or exclude the proffered evidence as required by the rule of law under which the question arises.

(b) If a preliminary fact is also a fact in issue in the action:

(1) The jury shall not be informed of the court's determination as to the existence or nonexistence of the preliminary fact.

(2) If the proffered evidence is admitted, the jury shall not be instructed to disregard

(b) Relevancy conditioned on fact.
When the relevancy of evidence depends upon the fulfillment of a condition of fact, the court shall admit it upon, or subject to, the introduction of evidence sufficient to support a finding of the fulfillment of the condition.

the evidence if its determination of the fact differs from the court's determination of the preliminary fact.

C.E.C. § 403. Determination of foundational and other preliminary facts where relevancy, personal knowledge, or authenticity is disputed
(a) The proponent of the proffered evidence has the burden of producing evidence as to the existence of the preliminary fact, and the proffered evidence is inadmissible unless the court finds that there is evidence sufficient to sustain a finding of the existence of the preliminary fact, when:
(1) The relevance of the proffered evidence depends on the existence of the preliminary fact;
(2) The preliminary fact is the personal knowledge of a witness concerning the subject matter of his testimony;
(3) The preliminary fact is the authenticity of a writing; or
(4) The proffered evidence is of a statement or other conduct of a particular person and the preliminary fact is whether that person made the statement or so conducted himself.
(b) Subject to Section 702, the court may admit conditionally the proffered evidence under this section, subject to evidence of the preliminary fact being supplied later in the course of the trial.
(c) If the court admits the proffered evidence under this section, the court:
(1) May, and on request shall, instruct the jury to determine whether the preliminary fact exists and to disregard the proffered evidence unless the jury finds that the preliminary fact does exist.
(2) Shall instruct the jury to disregard the proffered evidence if the court subsequently determines that a jury could not reasonably find that the preliminary fact exists.

(c) Hearing of jury. Hearings on the admissibility of confessions shall in all cases be conducted out of the hearing of the jury. Hearings on other preliminary matters shall be so conducted when the interests of justice require, or when an accused is a witness and so requests.

(d) Testimony by accused. The accused does not, by testifying upon a preliminary matter, become subject to cross-examination as to other issues in the case.

(e) Weight and credibility. This rule does not limit the right of a party to introduce before the jury evidence relevant to weight or credibility.

C.E.C. § 402. Procedure for determining foundational and other preliminary facts
(a) When the existence of a preliminary fact is disputed, its existence or nonexistence shall be determined as provided in this article.
(b) The court may hear and determine the question of the admissibility of evidence out of the presence or hearing of the jury; but in a criminal action, the court shall hear and determine the question of the admissibility of a confession or admission of the defendant out of the presence and hearing of the jury if any party so requests.
(c) A ruling on the admissibility of evidence implies whatever finding of fact is prerequisite thereto; a separate or formal finding is unnecessary unless required by statute.

C.E.C. § 406. Evidence affecting weight or credibility
This article does not limit the right of a party to introduce before the trier of fact evidence relevant to weight or credibility.

1. Action for personal injuries arising out of an automobile accident. Plaintiff offers the testimony of a witness who says she heard defendant say, "I ran the red light." Defendant will deny ever having made that statement. Both Federal and California evidence law will consider this evidence inadmissible hearsay unless it is deemed to be a statement by the defendant. Is the identity of the speaker a preliminary fact to be decided under Rule 104(a) or Rule 104(b)? Under C.E.C. § 403 or 405? Why does it matter?

2. Same case. Plaintiff offers the testimony of a witness who says she heard a bystander at the accident scene shout, "That Chevy just ran the red light! I'm so excited!" Both Federal and California evidence law will consider this evidence inadmissible hearsay unless it is deemed to be a statement by a witness who was speaking while under the stress of excitement. Is the emotional state of the speaker a preliminary fact to be decided under Rule 104(a) or Rule 104(b)? Under C.E.C. § 403 or 405? Can the court consider the statement itself in deciding this fact?

CHAPTER
3

The Hearsay Rule

B.   THE RULE

Fed. R. Evid. 801. Definitions
The following definitions apply under this article:
(a) Statement. A "statement" is (1) an oral or written assertion or (2) nonverbal conduct of a person, if it is intended by the person as an assertion.

C.E.C. § 225. Statement
"Statement" means (a) oral or written verbal expression or (b) nonverbal conduct of a person intended by him as a substitute for oral or written verbal expression.

C.E.C. § 125. Conduct
"Conduct" includes all active and passive behavior, both verbal and nonverbal.

(b) Declarant. A "declarant" is a person who makes a statement.

C.E.C. § 135. Declarant
"Declarant" is a person who makes a statement.

(c) Hearsay. "Hearsay" is a statement, other than one made by the declarant while testifying at the trial or hearing, offered in evidence to prove the truth of the matter asserted.

C.E.C. § 1200. The hearsay rule
(a) "Hearsay evidence" is evidence of a statement that was made other than by a witness while testifying at the hearing and that is offered to prove the truth of the matter stated.

C.E.C. § 145. The hearing
"The hearing" means the hearing at which a question under this code arises, and not some earlier or later hearing.

Fed. R. Evid. 802. Hearsay Rule
Hearsay is not admissible except as provided by these rules or by other rules prescribed by the Supreme Court pursuant to statutory authority or by Act of Congress.

C.E.C. § 1200. The hearsay rule
(b) Except as provided by law, hearsay evidence is inadmissible.
(c) This section shall be known and may be cited as the hearsay rule.

F.   HEARSAY WITHIN HEARSAY

Fed. R. Evid. 805. Hearsay Within Hearsay	C.E.C. § 1201. Multiple hearsay
Hearsay included within hearsay is not excluded under the hearsay rule if each part of the combined statements conforms with an exception to the hearsay rule provided in these rules.	A statement within the scope of an exception to the hearsay rule is not inadmissible on the ground that the evidence of such statement is hearsay evidence if such hearsay evidence consists of one or more statements each of which meets the requirements of an exception to the hearsay rule.

J.   EXEMPTIONS FROM THE HEARSAY RULE: PARTY ADMISSIONS

Fed. R. Evid. 801. Definitions	C.E.C. § 1220. Admission of party
(d) Statements which are not hearsay. A statement is not hearsay if— (2) Admission by party-opponent. The statement is offered against a party and is (A) the party's own statement, in either an individual or a representative capacity or	Evidence of a statement is not made inadmissible by the hearsay rule when offered against the declarant in an action to which he is a party in either his individual or representative capacity, regardless of whether the statement was made in his individual or representative capacity.

(B) a statement of which the party has manifested an adoption or belief in its truth, or	**C.E.C. § 1221. Adoptive admission** Evidence of a statement offered against a party is not made inadmissible by the hearsay rule if the statement is one of which the party, with knowledge of the content thereof, has by words or other conduct manifested his adoption or his belief in its truth.
(C) a statement by a person authorized by the party to make a statement concerning the subject, or	**C.E.C. § 1222. Authorized admission** Evidence of a statement offered against a party is not made inadmissible by the hearsay rule if: (a) The statement was made by a person authorized by the party to make a statement or statements for him concerning the subject matter of the statement; and (b) The evidence is offered either after admission of evidence sufficient to sustain a finding of such authority or, in the court's discretion as to the order of proof, subject to the admission of such evidence.
(D) a statement by the party's agent or servant concerning a matter within the scope of the agency or employment, made during the existence of the relationship, or	**C.E.C. § 1224. Statement of declarant whose liability or breach of duty is in issue** When the liability, obligation, or duty of a party to a civil action is based in whole or in part upon the liability, obligation, or duty of the declarant, or when the claim or right asserted by a party to a civil action is barred or diminished by a breach of duty by the declarant, evidence of a statement made by the declarant is as admissible against the party as it would be if offered against the declarant in an action involving that liability, obligation, duty, or breach of duty.
	C.E.C. § 1225. Statement of declarant whose right or title is in issue When a right, title, or interest in any property or claim asserted by a party to a civil action requires a determination that a right, title, or interest exists or existed in

the declarant, evidence of a statement made by the declarant during the time the party now claims the declarant was the holder of the right, title, or interest is as admissible against the party as it would be if offered against the declarant in an action involving that right, title, or interest.

C.E.C. § 1227. Statement of declarant in action for his wrongful death
Evidence of a statement by the deceased is not made inadmissible by the hearsay rule if offered against the plaintiff in an action for wrongful death brought under Section 377 of the Code of Civil Procedure.

C.E.C. § 1223. Admission of co-conspirator
Evidence of a statement offered against a party is not made inadmissible by the hearsay rule if:
(a) The statement was made by the declarant while participating in a conspiracy to commit a crime or civil wrong and in furtherance of the objective of that conspiracy;
(b) The statement was made prior to or during the time that the party was participating in that conspiracy; and
(c) The evidence is offered either after admission of evidence sufficient to sustain a finding of the facts specified in subdivisions (a) and (b) or, in the court's discretion as to the order of proof, subject to the admission of such evidence.

(E) a statement by a coconspirator of a party during the course and in furtherance of the conspiracy.

The contents of the statement shall be considered but are not alone sufficient to establish the declarant's authority under subdivision (C), the agency or employment relationship and scope thereof under subdivision (D), or the existence of the conspiracy and the participation therein of the declarant and the party against whom the statement is offered under subdivision (E).

Fed. R. Evid. 106. Remainder of or Related Writings or Recorded Statements	C.E.C. § 356. Entire act, declaration, conversation, or writing to elucidate part offered
When a writing or recorded statement or part thereof is introduced by a party, an adverse party may require the introduction at that time of any other part or any other writing or recorded statement which ought in fairness to be considered contemporaneously with it.	Where part of an act, declaration, conversation, or writing is given in evidence by one party, the whole on the same subject may be inquired into by an adverse party; when a letter is read, the answer may be given; and when a detached act, declaration, conversation, or writing is given in evidence, any other act, declaration, conversation, or writing which is necessary to make it understood may also be given in evidence.

Questions for Classroom Discussion
Casebook page 187

1. Action for breach of contract brought in federal court. Plaintiff offers the out of court statement of defendant "I breached the contract." Defendant objects on the ground of hearsay. Should the court admit the evidence on the ground it is not hearsay or on the ground it is hearsay but within an exception to the hearsay rule? If the evidence is offered in a California superior court, is the answer different?

2. Same case. After defendant's statement is admitted, defendant offers evidence that, immediately after defendant said, "I breached the contract," he added, "but not before plaintiff refused to perform as promised." Is the rest of defendant's statement admissible under the Federal Rules over a hearsay objection? If the evidence is offered in a California superior court, is the answer different?

3. Prosecution for bank robbery and conspiracy. The prosecution offers into evidence the out-of-court statement of one of the alleged members of the gang made to another member of the gang while planning the robbery, "You don't need to worry about the cops. Joe [defendant's name] is our getaway driver and he is the best in the business." Defendant objects on the ground of hearsay. The prosecution argues that the statement is an admission of a co-conspirator. For purposes of admitting this evidence under the Federal Rules, what is the prosecution's burden of proof for showing the existence of a conspiracy? May the court consider the statement itself in determining whether a conspiracy existed for purposes of deciding whether the statement is a co-conspirator admission? What are the answers to these questions under the C.E.C.?

K. EXEMPTIONS FROM THE HEARSAY RULE: PRIOR STATEMENTS OF WITNESSES

Fed. R. Evid. 801. Definitions (d) Statements which are not hearsay. A statement is not hearsay if— (1) Prior statement by witness. The declarant testifies at the trial or hearing and is subject to cross-examination concerning the statement, and the statement is	
(A) inconsistent with the declarant's testimony, and was given under oath subject to the penalty of perjury at a trial, hearing, or other proceeding, or in a deposition, or	**C.E.C. § 1235. Inconsistent statements** Evidence of a statement made by a witness is not made inadmissible by the hearsay rule if the statement is inconsistent with his testimony at the hearing and is offered in compliance with Section 770.
(B) consistent with the declarant's testimony and is offered to rebut an express or implied charge against the declarant of recent fabrication or improper influence or motive, or	**C.E.C. § 1236. Prior consistent statements** Evidence of a statement previously made by a witness is not made inadmissible by the hearsay rule if the statement is consistent with his testimony at the hearing and is offered in compliance with Section 791.
(C) one of identification of a person made after perceiving the person;	**C.E.C. § 1238. Prior identification** Evidence of a statement previously made by a witness is not made inadmissible by the hearsay rule if the statement would have been admissible if made by him while testifying and: (a) The statement is an identification of a party or another as a person who participated in a crime or other occurrence; (b) The statement was made at a time when the crime or other occurrence was fresh in the witness' memory; and (c) The evidence of the statement is offered after the witness testifies that he made the identification and that it was a true reflection of his opinion at that time.

Murder prosecution. Prosecution calls Witness, who testifies that he was present at the scene of the crime and that defendant was the perpetrator. The defense does not cross-examine. Prosecution then calls Police Officer who testifies that, over a year after the killing, defendant was apprehended and placed in a police lineup during which Witness pointed at defendant and said, "That's your man!" Defendant objects on the ground of hearsay. What result under the Federal Rules? The C.E.C.?

M.   EXCEPTIONS TO THE HEARSAY RULE: AVAILABILITY OF DECLARANT IMMATERIAL

1.   *Time-Sensitive Statements (Rules 803(1) and (2))*

Fed. R. Evid. 803. Hearsay Exceptions; Availability of Declarant Immaterial	
The following are not excluded by the hearsay rule, even though the declarant is available as a witness:	
(1) Present sense impression. A statement describing or explaining an event or condition made while the declarant was perceiving the event or condition, or immediately thereafter.	**C.E.C. § 1241. Contemporaneous statement** Evidence of a statement is not made inadmissible by the hearsay rule if the statement: (a) Is offered to explain, qualify, or make understandable conduct of the declarant; and (b) Was made while the declarant was engaged in such conduct.
(2) Excited utterance. A statement relating to a startling event or condition made while the declarant was under the stress of excitement caused by the event or condition.	**C.E.C. § 1240. Spontaneous statement** Evidence of a statement is not made``` inadmissible by the hearsay rule if the statement: (a) Purports to narrate, describe, or explain an act, condition, or event perceived by the declarant; and (b) Was made spontaneously while the declarant was under the stress of excitement caused by such perception.

	C.E.C. § 1370. Threat of infliction of injury
	(a) Evidence of a statement by a declarant is not made inadmissible by the hearsay rule if all of the following conditions are met: (1) The statement purports to narrate, describe, or explain the infliction or threat of physical injury upon the declarant. (2) The declarant is unavailable as a witness pursuant to Section 240. (3) The statement was made at or near the time of the infliction or threat of physical injury. Evidence of statements made more than five years before the filing of the current action or proceeding shall be inadmissible under this section. (4) The statement was made under circumstances that would indicate its trustworthiness. (5) The statement was made in writing, was electronically recorded, or made to a physician, nurse, paramedic, or to a law enforcement official. (b) For purposes of paragraph (4) of subdivision (a), circumstances relevant to the issue of trustworthiness include, but are not limited to, the following: (1) Whether the statement was made in contemplation of pending or anticipated litigation in which the declarant was interested. (2) Whether the declarant has a bias or motive for fabricating the statement, and the extent of any bias or motive. (3) Whether the statement is corroborated by evidence other than statements that are admissible only pursuant to this section. (c) A statement is admissible pursuant to this section only if the proponent of the statement makes known to the adverse party the intention to offer the statement and the particulars of the statement sufficiently in advance of the proceedings in order to provide the adverse party with a fair opportunity to prepare to meet the statement.

1. [The following is question 7 from page 202 of the casebook.] Prosecution of Defendant for the murder of Victim. Defendant claims he was in another town on the day of the murder. The prosecution calls Witness to testify that he was talking to Victim on the telephone on the day of the murder when Victim said, "Defendant just walked into the room. It looks like he wants to show me his new chainsaw. I will call you right back." He never did. Defendant objects on hearsay grounds. How should the court rule under the Federal Rules? The C.E.C.?

2. Same case. The prosecution offers into evidence the sound recording of a telephone call the victim made to 911 in which she stated, in a calm voice, "My former husband kicked me in the head a few minutes ago." When the police arrived shortly thereafter, they discovered the victim unconscious. She subsequently died of a brain hemorrhage. Defendant objects on hearsay grounds. How should the court rule under the Federal Rules? The C.E.C.?

Fed. R. Evid. 803. Hearsay Exceptions; Availability of Declarant Immaterial

The following are not excluded by the hearsay rule, even though the declarant is available as a witness:

(3) Then existing mental, emotional, or physical condition. A statement of the declarant's then existing state of mind, emotion, sensation, or physical condition (such as intent, plan, motive, design, mental feeling, pain, and bodily health), but not including a statement of memory or belief to prove the fact remembered or believed unless it relates to the execution, revocation, identification, or terms of declarant's will.

C.E.C. § 1250. Statement of declarant's then existing mental or physical state

(a) Subject to Section 1252, evidence of a statement of the declarant's then existing state of mind, emotion, or physical sensation (including a statement of intent, plan, motive, design, mental feeling, pain, or bodily health) is not made inadmissible by the hearsay rule when:

(1) The evidence is offered to prove the declarant's state of mind, emotion, or physical sensation at that time or at any other time when it is itself an issue in the action; or

(2) The evidence is offered to prove or explain acts or conduct of the declarant.

(b) This section does not make admissible evidence of a statement of memory or belief to prove the fact remembered or believed.

C.E.C. § 1260. Statement concerning declarant's will

(a) Evidence of a statement made by a declarant who is unavailable as a witness that he has or has not made a will, or has or has not revoked his will, or that identifies his will, is not made inadmissible by the hearsay rule.

(b) Evidence of a statement is inadmissible under this section if the statement was made under circumstances such as to indicate its lack of trustworthiness.

C.E.C. § 1251. Statement of declarant's previously existing mental or physical state

Subject to Section 1252, evidence of a statement of the declarant's state of mind, emotion, or physical sensation (including a statement of intent, plan, motive, design, mental feeling, pain, or bodily health) at a time prior to the statement is not made inadmissible by the hearsay rule if:

(a) The declarant is unavailable as a witness; and

(b) The evidence is offered to prove such prior state of mind, emotion, or physical sensation when it is itself an issue in the action and the evidence is not offered to prove any fact other than such state of mind, emotion, or physical sensation.

C.E.C. § 1252. Restriction on admissibility of statement of mental or physical state

Evidence of a statement is inadmissible under this article if the statement was made under circumstances such as to indicate its lack of trustworthiness.

C.E.C. § 1261. Statement of decedent offered in action against his estate

(a) Evidence of a statement is not made inadmissible by the hearsay rule when offered in an action upon a claim or demand against the estate of the declarant if the statement was made upon the personal knowledge of the declarant at a time when the matter had been recently perceived by him and while his recollection was clear.

(b) Evidence of a statement is inadmissible under this section if the statement was made under circumstances such as to indicate its lack of trustworthiness.

(4) **Statements for purposes of medical diagnosis or treatment.** Statements made for purposes of medical diagnosis or treatment and describing medical history, or past or present symptoms, pain, or sensations, or the inception or general character of the cause or external source thereof insofar as reasonably pertinent to diagnosis or treatment.	**C.E.C. § 1253. Statements for purposes of medical diagnosis or treatment; contents of statement; child abuse or neglect; age limitations** Subject to Section 1252, evidence of a statement is not made inadmissible by the hearsay rule if the statement was made for purposes of medical diagnosis or treatment and describes medical history, or past or present symptoms, pain, or sensations, or the inception or general character of the cause or external source thereof insofar as reasonably pertinent to diagnosis or treatment. This section applies only to a statement made by a victim who is a minor at the time of the proceedings, provided the statement was made when the victim was under the age of 12 describing any act, or attempted act, of child abuse or neglect. "Child abuse" and "child neglect," for purposes of this section, have the meanings provided in subdivision (c) of Section 1360. In addition, "child abuse" means any act proscribed by Chapter 5 (commencing with Section 281) of Title 9 of Part 1 of the Penal Code committed against a minor.

Questions for Classroom Discussion
Casebook page 213

1. [The following is based on question 2 from page 213 of the casebook.] Personal injury action by Plaintiff against Defendant following an auto collision. To prove Plaintiff suffered injuries in the collision, Plaintiff calls Witness to testify that at the scene, when Witness asked Plaintiff if she was hurt, Plaintiff said, "My leg is killing me." Is the statement admissible under the Federal Rules or the C.E.C.?

2. [The following is based on question 3 from page 213 of the casebook.] Same case. Suppose that in response to Witness's question, Plaintiff added, "I was feeling fine just before the accident." Plaintiff is unavailable to testify. Is the statement admissible under the Federal Rules or the C.E.C.?

3. Same case. Suppose that Plaintiff's statement in the preceding question was given to a paramedic who, upon arriving at the accident scene, asked Plaintiff about his general medical condition prior to the accident. Assume that Plaintiff is available to testify. Is the statement admissible under the Federal Rules or the C.E.C.?

Fed. R. Evid. 803. Hearsay Exceptions; Availability of Declarant Immaterial

The following are not excluded by the hearsay rule, even though the declarant is available as a witness:

(5) Recorded recollection. A memorandum or record concerning a matter about which a witness once had knowledge but now has insufficient recollection to enable the witness to testify fully and accurately, shown to have been made or adopted by the witness when the matter was fresh in the witness' memory and to reflect that knowledge correctly. If admitted, the memorandum or record may be read into evidence but may not itself be received as an exhibit unless offered by an adverse party.

C.E.C. § 1237. Past recollection recorded

(a) Evidence of a statement previously made by a witness is not made inadmissible by the hearsay rule if the statement would have been admissible if made by him while testifying, the statement concerns a matter as to which the witness has insufficient present recollection to enable him to testify fully and accurately, and the statement is contained in a writing which:
(1) Was made at a time when the fact recorded in the writing actually occurred or was fresh in the witness' memory;
(2) Was made (i) by the witness himself or under his direction or (ii) by some other person for the purpose of recording the witness' statement at the time it was made;
(3) Is offered after the witness testifies that the statement he made was a true statement of such fact; and
(4) Is offered after the writing is authenticated as an accurate record of the statement.
(b) The writing may be read into evidence, but the writing itself may not be received in evidence unless offered by an adverse party.

Fed. R. Evid. 612. Writing Used to Refresh Memory

Except as otherwise provided in criminal proceedings by section 3500 of title 18, United States Code, if a witness uses a writing to refresh memory for the purpose of testifying, either—
(1) while testifying, or
(2) before testifying, if the court in its discretion determines it is necessary in the interests of justice, an adverse party is entitled to have the writing produced at the

C.E.C. § 771. Production of writing used to refresh memory
(a) Subject to subdivision (c), if a witness, either while testifying or prior thereto, uses a writing to refresh his memory with respect to any matter about which he testifies, such writing must be produced at the hearing at the request of an adverse party and, unless the writing is so produced, the testimony of the witness concerning such matter shall be stricken.
(b) If the writing is produced at the hearing, the adverse party may, if he chooses,

hearing, to inspect it, to cross-examine the witness thereon, and to introduce in evidence those portions which relate to the testimony of the witness. If it is claimed that the writing contains matters not related to the subject matter of the testimony the court shall examine the writing in camera, excise any portions not so related, and order delivery of the remainder to the party entitled thereto. Any portion withheld over objections shall be preserved and made available to the appellate court in the event of an appeal. If a writing is not produced or delivered pursuant to order under this rule, the court shall make any order justice requires, except that in criminal cases when the prosecution elects not to comply, the order shall be one striking the testimony or, if the court in its discretion determines that the interests of justice so require, declaring a mistrial.

inspect the writing, cross-examine the witness concerning it, and introduce in evidence such portion of it as may be pertinent to the testimony of the witness.
(c) Production of the writing is excused, and the testimony of the witness shall not be stricken, if the writing:
(1) Is not in the possession or control of the witness or the party who produced his testimony concerning the matter; and
(2) Was not reasonably procurable by such party through the use of the court's process or other available means.

Question for Classroom Discussion
Casebook page 222

Civil action for personal injuries. Plaintiff testifies that defendant sexually assaulted her. On cross-examination defendant reveals many inconsistencies between plaintiff's testimony and the statement she gave to the police shortly after the alleged assault. Plaintiff also admits during cross-examination that she reviewed her daily diary prior to testifying to help refresh her recollection. Defendant asks to have the diary produced and plaintiff objects, asserting that the diary contains personal reflections and other matters that would be embarrassing to reveal to others, especially defendant. Must the court order plaintiff to produce the diary? If the court orders the diary produced and plaintiff still declines, must the court strike her testimony? Answer according to the Federal Rules and the C.E.C.

Fed. R. Evid. 803. Hearsay Exceptions; Availability of Declarant Immaterial

The following are not excluded by the hearsay rule, even though the declarant is available as a witness:

(6) Records of Regularly Conducted Activity.—A memorandum, report, record, or data compilation, in any form, of acts, events, conditions, opinions, or diagnoses, made at or near the time by, or from information transmitted by, a person with knowledge, if kept in the course of a regularly conducted business activity, and if it was the regular practice of that business activity to make the memorandum, report, record or data compilation, all as shown by the testimony of the custodian or other qualified witness, or by certification that complies with Rule 902(11), Rule 902(12), or a statute permitting certification, unless the source of information or the method or circumstances of preparation indicate lack of trustworthiness. The term "business" as used in this paragraph includes business, institution, association, profession, occupation, and calling of every kind, whether or not conducted for profit.

(7) Absence of entry in records kept in accordance with the provisions of paragraph (6). Evidence that a matter is not included in the memoranda reports, records, or data compilations, in any form, kept in accordance with the provisions of paragraph (6), to prove the nonoccurrence or nonexistence of the matter, if the matter was of a kind of which a memorandum, report, record, or data compilation was regularly made and preserved, unless the sources of information or other circumstances indicate lack of trustworthiness.

C.E.C. § 1270. A business

As used in this article, "a business" includes every kind of business, governmental activity, profession, occupation, calling, or operation of institutions, whether carried on for profit or not.

C.E.C. § 1271. Admissible writings

Evidence of a writing made as a record of an act, condition, or event is not made inadmissible by the hearsay rule when offered to prove the act, condition, or event if:

(a) The writing was made in the regular course of a business;

(b) The writing was made at or near the time of the act, condition, or event;

(c) The custodian or other qualified witness testifies to its identity and the mode of its preparation; and

(d) The sources of information and method and time of preparation were such as to indicate its trustworthiness.

C.E.C. § 1272. Absence of entry in business records

Evidence of the absence from the records of a business of a record of an asserted act, condition, or event is not made inadmissible by the hearsay rule when offered to prove the nonoccurrence of the act or event, or the nonexistence of the condition, if:

(a) It was the regular course of that business to make records of all such acts, conditions, or events at or near the time of the act, condition, or event and to preserve them; and

	(b) The sources of information and method and time of preparation of the records of that business were such that the absence of a record of an act, condition, or event is a trustworthy indication that the act or event did not occur or the condition did not exist.
(8) Public records and reports. Records, reports, statements, or data compilations, in any form, of public offices or agencies, setting forth (A) the activities of the office or agency, or (B) matters observed pursuant to duty imposed by law as to which matters there was a duty to report, excluding, however, in criminal cases matters observed by police officers and other law enforcement personnel, or (C) in civil actions and proceedings and against the Government in criminal cases, factual findings resulting from an investigation made pursuant to authority granted by law, unless the sources of information or other circumstances indicate lack of trustworthiness.	**C.E.C. § 1280. Record by public employee** Evidence of a writing made as a record of an act, condition, or event is not made inadmissible by the hearsay rule when offered in any civil or criminal proceeding to prove the act, condition, or event if all of the following applies: (a) The writing was made by and within the scope of duty of a public employee. (b) The writing was made at or near the time of the act, condition, or event. (c) The sources of information and method and time of preparation were such as to indicate its trustworthiness.
(10) Absence of public record or entry. To prove the absence of a record, report, statement, or data compilation, in any form, or the nonoccurrence or nonexistence of a matter of which a record, report, statement, or data compilation, in any form, was regularly made and preserved by a public office or agency, evidence in the form of a certification in accordance with rule 902, or testimony, that diligent search failed to disclose the record, report, statement, or data compilation, or entry.	**C.E.C. § 1284. Statement of absence of public record** Evidence of a writing made by the public employee who is the official custodian of the records in a public office, reciting diligent search and failure to find a record, is not made inadmissible by the hearsay rule when offered to prove the absence of a record in that office.

N.   EXCEPTIONS TO THE HEARSAY RULE: UNAVAILABILITY OF DECLARANT REQUIRED

1.   *Unavailability*

Fed. R. Evid. 804. Hearsay Exceptions; Declarant Unavailable	**C.E.C. § 240. Unavailable as a witness**
(a) Definition of unavailability. "Unavailability as a witness" includes situations in which the declarant— (1) is exempted by ruling of the court on the ground of privilege from testifying concerning the subject matter of the declarant's statement; or (2) persists in refusing to testify concerning the subject matter of the declarant's statement despite an order of the court to do so; or (3) testifies to a lack of memory of the subject matter of the declarant's statement; or (4) is unable to be present or to testify at	(a) Except as otherwise provided in subdivision (b), "unavailable as a witness" means that the declarant is any of the following: (1) Exempted or precluded on the ground of privilege from testifying concerning the matter to which his or her statement is relevant. (2) Disqualified from testifying to the matter. (3) Dead or unable to attend or to testify at the hearing because of then existing physical or mental illness or infirmity. (4) Absent from the hearing and the court is unable to compel his or her attendance by its process.

the hearing because of death or then existing physical or mental illness or infirmity; or

(5) is absent from the hearing and the proponent of a statement has been unable to procure the declarant's attendance (or in the case of a hearsay exception under subdivision (b)(2), (3), or (4), the declarant's attendance or testimony) by process or other reasonable means.

A declarant is not unavailable as a witness if exemption, refusal, claim of lack of memory, inability, or absence is due to the procurement or wrongdoing of the proponent of a statement for the purpose of preventing the witness from attending or testifying.

(5) Absent from the hearing and the proponent of his or her statement has exercised reasonable diligence but has been unable to procure his or her attendance by the court's process.

(b) A declarant is not unavailable as a witness if the exemption, preclusion, disqualification, death, inability, or absence of the declarant was brought about by the procurement or wrongdoing of the proponent of his or her statement for the purpose of preventing the declarant from attending or testifying.

(c) Expert testimony which establishes that physical or mental trauma resulting from an alleged crime has caused harm to a witness of sufficient severity that the witness is physically unable to testify or is unable to testify without suffering substantial trauma may constitute a sufficient showing of unavailability pursuant to paragraph (3) of subdivision(a). As used in this section, the term "expert" means a physician and surgeon, including a psychiatrist, or any person described by subdivision (b), (c), or (e) of Section 1010. The introduction of evidence to establish the unavailability of a witness under this subdivision shall not be deemed procurement of unavailability, in absence of proof to the contrary.

Questions for Classroom Discussion
Casebook page 237

1. Prosecution for racketeering. The prosecution calls an alleged member of defendant's crime "family" to testify to the organization of the family's criminal enterprises. The witness refuses to take the stand despite a court order to testify. Is the witness "unavailable" under the Federal Rules? The C.E.C.?

2. Same case. The witness is willing to take the stand and testify, but refuses to take an oath or give an affirmation to testify truthfully. Is the witness "unavailable" under the Federal Rules? The C.E.C.?

3. Same case. The witness is sworn and takes the stand, but claims to remember nothing about the family's business. Is the witness "unavailable" under the Federal Rules? The C.E.C.?

4. Same case. The prosecution has been unable to serve the witness with a summons to appear at trial, notwithstanding repeated attempts to do so. The prosecutor knows the witness' cell phone number but never calls to ask if he would voluntarily appear. Is the witness "unavailable" under the Federal Rules? The C.E.C.?

5. Prosecution for child abuse. Witness is a ten year old child who the prosecution alleges was sexually abused and beaten by defendant. While the witness is in the courthouse, his psychiatrist testifies in a pretrial hearing that Witness is deathly afraid of defendant and, if made to testify in open court, will suffer significant psychological trauma. Is the witness "unavailable" under the Federal Rules? The C.E.C.?

2. *The Former Testimony Exception (FRE 804(b)(1))*

Fed. R. Evid. 804. Hearsay Exceptions; Declarant Unavailable	C.E.C. § 1290. Former testimony
(b) Hearsay exceptions. The following are not excluded by the hearsay rule if the declarant is unavailable as a witness: **(1) Former testimony.** Testimony given as a witness at another hearing of the same or a different proceeding, or in a deposition taken in compliance with law in the course of the same or another proceeding, if the party against whom the testimony is now offered, or, in a civil action or proceeding, a predecessor in interest, had an opportunity and similar motive to develop the testimony by direct, cross, or redirect examination.	As used in this article, "former testimony" means testimony given under oath in: (a) Another action or in a former hearing or trial of the same action; (b) A proceeding to determine a controversy conducted by or under the supervision of an agency that has the power to determine such a controversy and is an agency of the United States or a public entity in the United States; (c) A deposition taken in compliance with law in another action; or (d) An arbitration proceeding if the evidence of such former testimony is a verbatim transcript thereof.

C.E.C. § 1291. Former testimony offered against party to former proceeding

(a) Evidence of former testimony is not made inadmissible by the hearsay rule if the declarant is unavailable as a witness and:

(1) The former testimony is offered against a person who offered it in evidence in his own behalf on the former occasion or against the successor in interest of such person; or

(2) The party against whom the former testimony is offered was a party to the action or proceeding in which the testimony was given and had the right and opportunity to cross-examine the declarant with an interest and motive similar to that which he has at the hearing.

(b) The admissibility of former testimony under this section is subject to the same limitations and objections as though the declarant were testifying at the hearing, except that former testimony offered under this section is not subject to:

(1) Objections to the form of the question which were not made at the time the former testimony was given.

(2) Objections based on competency or privilege which did not exist at the time the former testimony was given.

C.E.C. § 1292. Former testimony offered against person not a party to former proceeding

(a) Evidence of former testimony is not made inadmissible by the hearsay rule if:

(1) The declarant is unavailable as a witness;

(2) The former testimony is offered in a civil action; and

(3) The issue is such that the party to the action or proceeding in which the former testimony was given had the right and opportunity to cross-examine the declarant with an interest and motive similar to that

	which the party against whom the testimony is offered has at the hearing. (b) The admissibility of former testimony under this section is subject to the same limitations and objections as though the declarant were testifying at the hearing, except that former testimony offered under this section is not subject to objections based on competency or privilege which did not exist at the time the former testimony was given.

Questions for Classroom Discussion
Casebook page 243

1. [The following is based on question 7 from page 243 of the casebook, with the query concerning the C.E.C.] Prosecution of Defendant for racketeering following a grand jury indictment. The prosecution called Witness to testify before the grand jury but, to the prosecution's surprise, the Witness testified that defendant had no involvement in the alleged racketeering. Other witnesses, however, provide sufficient evidence to lead the grand jury to indict Defendant. Witness dies in a plane crash before trial, due to no fault of the prosecution or Defendant. At trial, Defendant offers into evidence the transcript of Witness's grand jury testimony. The prosecution objects on hearsay grounds. Should the objection be sustained under the Federal Rules? The C.E.C.?

2. Civil action for breach of contract. Plaintiff conducted a deposition in this case of one of defendant's employees. The witness is unavailable at trial and plaintiff offers the testimony into evidence. Defendant was present at the deposition and examined the witness extensively. Defendant objects on the ground of hearsay. Is the deposition testimony admissible under Rule 804(b)(1)? C.E.C. § 1291?

Fed. R. Evid. 804. Hearsay Exceptions; Declarant Unavailable	C.E.C. § 1242. Dying declaration
(b) Hearsay exceptions. The following are not excluded by the hearsay rule if the declarant is unavailable as a witness: **(2) Statement under belief of impending death.** In a prosecution for homicide or in a civil action or proceeding, a statement made by a declarant while believing that the declarant's death was imminent, concerning the cause or circumstances of what the declarant believed to be impending death.	Evidence of a statement made by a dying person respecting the cause and circumstances of his death is not made inadmissible by the hearsay rule if the statement was made upon his personal knowledge and under a sense of immediately impending death.

Question for Classroom Discussion
Casebook Page 247

[The following is based on question 7 from page 247 of the casebook.] Prosecution of Defendant for the attempted murder of Victim. Defendant denies involvement. The attack on Victim left her critically injured and she lapsed into a coma from which she has not recovered at the time of trial. The prosecution wishes to offer evidence that before becoming comatose, Victim told an attending nurse, "I don't expect to make it. I hope Defendant pays for this." Defendant objects on hearsay grounds. Should the objection be sustained under the Federal Rules? The C.E.C.?

Fed. R. Evid. 804. Hearsay Exceptions; Declarant Unavailable	**C.E.C. § 1230. Declarations against interest**
(b) Hearsay exceptions. The following are not excluded by the hearsay rule if the declarant is unavailable as a witness: **(3) Statement against interest.** A statement which was at the time of its making so far contrary to the declarant's pecuniary or proprietary interest, or so far tended to subject the declarant to civil or criminal liability, or to render invalid a claim by the declarant against another, that a reasonable person in the declarant's position would not have made the statement unless believing it to be true. A statement tending to expose the declarant to criminal liability and offered to exculpate the accused is not admissible unless corroborating circumstances clearly indicate the trustworthiness of the statement.	Evidence of a statement by a declarant having sufficient knowledge of the subject is not made inadmissible by the hearsay rule if the declarant is unavailable as a witness and the statement, when made, was so far contrary to the declarant's pecuniary or proprietary interest, or so far subjected him to the risk of civil or criminal liability, or so far tended to render invalid a claim by him against another, or created such a risk of making him an object of hatred, ridicule, or social disgrace in the community, that a reasonable man in his position would not have made the statement unless he believed it to be true.

Question for Classroom Discussion
Casebook Page 252

Murder prosecution. The victim was a member of the clergy. The defense offers into evidence a note shown to be in the victim's handwriting that reads, "I have swallowed a bottle of poison because I have lost my faith." The prosecution objects on hearsay grounds. Should the objection be sustained under the Federal Rules? The C.E.C.?

Fed. R. Evid. 804. Hearsay Exceptions; Declarant Unavailable	**C.E.C. § 1350. Unavailable declarant; hearsay rule**
(b) Hearsay exceptions. The following are not excluded by the hearsay rule if the declarant is unavailable as a witness: **(6) Forfeiture by wrongdoing.** A statement offered against a party that has engaged or acquiesced in wrongdoing that was intended to, and did, procure the unavailability of the declarant as a witness.	(a) In a criminal proceeding charging a serious felony, evidence of a statement made by a declarant is not made inadmissible by the hearsay rule if the declarant is unavailable as a witness, and all of the following are true: (1) There is clear and convincing evidence that the declarant's unavailability was knowingly caused by, aided by, or solicited by the party against whom the statement is offered for the purpose of preventing the arrest or prosecution of the party and is the result of the death by homicide or the kidnapping of the declarant. (2) There is no evidence that the unavailability of the declarant was caused by, aided by, solicited by, or procured on behalf of, the party who is offering the statement. (3) The statement has been memorialized in a tape recording made by a law enforcement official, or in a written statement prepared by a law enforcement official and signed by the declarant and notarized in the presence of the law enforcement official, prior to the death or kidnapping of the declarant. (4) The statement was made under circumstances which indicate its trustworthiness and was not the result of promise, inducement, threat, or coercion. (5) The statement is relevant to the issues to be tried (6) The statement is corroborated by other evidence which tends to connect the party against whom the statement is offered with the commission of the serious felony with which the party is charged. The corroboration is not sufficient if it merely shows the commission of the offense or the circumstances thereof.

(b) If the prosecution intends to offer a statement pursuant to this section, the prosecution shall serve a written notice upon the defendant at least 10 days prior to the hearing or trial at which the prosecution intends to offer the statement, unless the prosecution shows good cause for the failure to provide that notice. In the event that good cause is shown, the defendant shall be entitled to a reasonable continuance of the hearing or trial.

(c) If the statement is offered during trial, the court's determination shall be made out of the presence of the jury. If the defendant elects to testify at the hearing on a motion brought pursuant to this section, the court shall exclude from the examination every person except the clerk, the court reporter, the bailiff, the prosecutor, the investigating officer, the defendant and his or her counsel, an investigator for the defendant, and the officer having custody of the defendant. Notwithstanding any other provision of law, the defendant's testimony at the hearing shall not be admissible in any other proceeding except the hearing brought on the motion pursuant to this section. If a transcript is made of the defendant's testimony, it shall be sealed and transmitted to the clerk of the court in which the action is pending.

(d) As used in this section, "serious felony" means any of the felonies listed in subdivision (c) of Section 1192.7 of the Penal Code or any violation of Section 11351, 11352, 11378, or 11379 of the Health and Safety Code.

(e) If a statement to be admitted pursuant to this section includes hearsay statements made by anyone other than the declarant who is unavailable pursuant to subdivision (a), those hearsay statements are inadmissible unless they meet the requirements of an exception to the hearsay rule.

[The following is based on question 1 from page 264 of the casebook.] Negligence action by Plaintiff against Defendant arising from an automobile collision. Witness observed the collision, and Plaintiff plans to call Witness to testify at trial. Prior to trial, Defendant pays Witness to "disappear" for a while, making Witness unavailable to testify at the trial. Plaintiff wishes to offer into evidence Witness's statement to a police officer the day after the accident, in which Witness said that Defendant ran a red light and struck Plaintiff. Defendant objects on hearsay grounds. How should the court rule under the Federal Rules? Under the C.E.C.?

O.   THE RESIDUAL EXCEPTION (RULE 807)

Fed. R. Evid. 807. Residual Exception

A statement not specifically covered by Rule 803 or 804 but having equivalent circumstantial guarantees of trustworthiness, is not excluded by the hearsay rule, if the court determines that (A) the statement is offered as evidence of a material fact; (B) the statement is more probative on the point for which it is offered than any other evidence which the proponent can procure through reasonable efforts; and (C) the general purposes of these rules and the interests of justice will best be served by admission of the statement into evidence. However, a statement may not be admitted under this exception unless the proponent of it makes known to the adverse party sufficiently in advance of the trial or hearing to provide the adverse party with a fair opportunity to prepare to meet it, the proponent's intention to offer the statement and the particulars of it, including the name and address of the declarant.

C.E.C. § 1228. Admissibility of certain out-of-court statements of minors under the age of 12; establishing elements of certain sexually oriented crimes; notice to defendant

Notwithstanding any other provision of law, for the purpose of establishing the elements of the crime in order to admit as evidence the confession of a person accused of violating Section 261, 264.1, 285, 286, 288, 288a, 289, or 647a of the Penal Code, a court, in its discretion, may determine that a statement of the complaining witness is not made inadmissible by the hearsay rule if it finds all of the following:

(a) The statement was made by a minor child under the age of 12, and the contents of the statement were included in a written report of a law enforcement official or an employee of a county welfare department.

(b) The statement describes the minor child as a victim of sexual abuse.

(c) The statement was made prior to the defendant's confession. The court shall view with caution the testimony of a person recounting hearsay where there is evidence of personal bias or prejudice.

(d) There are no circumstances, such as significant inconsistencies between the confession and the statement concerning material facts establishing any element of the crime or the identification of the defendant, that would render the statement unreliable.

(e) The minor child is found to be unavailable pursuant to paragraph (2) or (3) of subdivision (a) of Section 240 or refuses to testify.

(f) The confession was memorialized in a trustworthy fashion by a law enforcement official.

If the prosecution intends to offer a statement of the complaining witness pursuant to this section, the prosecution shall serve a written notice upon the

	defendant at least 10 days prior to the hearing or trial at which the prosecution intends to offer the statement.
	If the statement is offered during trial, the court's determination shall be made out of the presence of the jury. If the statement is found to be admissible pursuant to this section, it shall be admitted out of the presence of the jury and solely for the purpose of determining the admissibility of the confession of the defendant.

Question for Classroom Discussion
Casebook Page 280

Prosecution for child molestation. Defendant consistently has denied the charges from the moment of his arrest. The prosecution offers into evidence the out of court statement of the child in question in which the child told a police officer that she was molested by defendant. Admissible over a hearsay objection under the Federal Rules? Under the C.E.C.?

P. MISCELLANEOUS EXCEPTIONS

1. Records of Vital Statistics (Rule 803(9)), Religious Organizations (Rule 803(11), and Marriage, Baptismal, and Similar Certificates (Rule 803(12))

Fed. R. Evid. 803. Hearsay Exceptions; Availability of Declarant Immaterial

The following are not excluded by the hearsay rule, even though the declarant is available as a witness:

(9) Records of vital statistics. Records or data compilations, in any form, of births, fetal deaths, deaths, or marriages, if the report thereof was made to a public office pursuant to requirements of law.

C.E.C. § 1281. Vital statistics records

Evidence of a writing made as a record of a birth, fetal death, death, or marriage is not made inadmissible by the hearsay rule if the maker was required by law to file the writing in a designated public office and the writing was made and filed as required by law.

(11) Records of religious organizations. Statements of births, marriages, divorces, deaths, legitimacy, ancestry, relationship by blood or marriage, or other similar facts of personal or family history, contained in a regularly kept record of a religious organization.

C.E.C. § 1315. Church records concerning family history

Evidence of a statement concerning a person's birth, marriage, divorce, death, parent and child relationship, race, ancestry, relationship by blood or marriage, or other similar fact of family history which is contained in a writing made as a record of a church, religious denomination, or religious society is not made inadmissible by the hearsay rule if:
(a) The statement is contained in a writing made as a record of an act, condition, or event that would be admissible as evidence of such act, condition, or event under Section 1271; and
(b) The statement is of a kind customarily recorded in connection with the act, condition, or event recorded in the writing.

(12) Marriage, baptismal, and similar certificates. Statements of fact contained in a certificate that the maker performed a marriage or other ceremony or administered a sacrament, made by a

C.E.C. § 1316. Marriage, baptismal and similar certificates

Evidence of a statement concerning a person's birth, marriage, divorce, death, parent and child relationship, race, ancestry, relationship by blood or marriage, clergyman, public official, or other person authorized by the rules or practices of a religious organization or by law to perform the act certified, and purporting to have been issued at the time of the act or within a reasonable time hereafter.

or other similar fact of family history is not made inadmissible by the hearsay rule if the statement is contained in a certificate that the maker thereof performed a marriage or other ceremony or administered a sacrament and:
(a) The maker was a clergyman, civil officer, or other person authorized to perform the acts reported in the certificate by law or by the rules, regulations, or requirements of a church, religious denomination, or religious society; and
(b) The certificate was issued by the maker at the time and place of the ceremony or sacrament or within a reasonable time thereafter.

2. Family Records (Rule 803(13)) and Statements of Personal or Family History (Rule 804(B)(4))

Fed. R. Evid. 803. Hearsay Exceptions; Availability of Declarant Immaterial
The following are not excluded by the hearsay rule, even though the declarant is available as a witness:

(13) Family records. Statements of fact concerning personal or family history contained in family Bibles, genealogies, charts, engravings on rings, inscriptions on family portraits, engravings on urns, crypts, or tombstones, or the like.

Fed. R. Evid. 804. Hearsay Exceptions; Declarant Unavailable
(b) Hearsay exceptions. The following are not excluded by the hearsay rule if the declarant is unavailable as a witness:
(4) Statement of personal or family history. (A) A statement concerning the declarant's own birth, adoption, marriage, divorce, legitimacy, relationship by blood, adoption, or marriage, ancestry, or other

C.E.C. § 1313. Reputation in family concerning family history
Evidence of reputation among members of a family is not made inadmissible by the hearsay rule if the reputation concerns the birth, marriage, divorce, death, parent and child relationship, race, ancestry, relationship by blood or marriage, or other similar fact of the family history of a member of the family by blood or marriage.

C.E.C. § 1310. Statement concerning declarant's own family history
(a) Subject to subdivision (b), evidence of a statement by a declarant who is unavailable as a witness concerning his own birth,

similar fact of personal or family history, even though declarant had no means of acquiring personal knowledge of the matter stated; or (B) a statement concerning the foregoing matters, and death also, of another person, if the declarant was related to the other by blood, adoption, or marriage or was so intimately associated with the other's family as to be likely to have accurate information concerning the matter declared.	marriage, divorce, a parent and child relationship, relationship by blood or marriage, race, ancestry, or other similar fact of his family history is not made inadmissible by the hearsay rule, even though the declarant had no means of acquiring personal knowledge of the matter declared. (b) Evidence of a statement is inadmissible under this section if the statement was made under circumstances such as to indicate its lack of trustworthiness.

3. Records of Documents Affecting an Interest in Property (Rule 803(14)) and Statements in Such Documents (Rule 803(15))

Fed. R. Evid. 803. Hearsay Exceptions; Availability of Declarant Immaterial The following are not excluded by the hearsay rule, even though the declarant is available as a witness:	
(14) Records of documents affecting an interest in property. The record of a document purporting to establish or affect an interest in property, as proof of the content of the original recorded document and its execution and delivery by each person by whom it purports to have been executed, if the record is a record of a public office and an applicable statute authorizes the recording of documents of that kind in that office.	**C.E.C. 1312. Entries in family records and the like** Evidence of entries in family Bibles or other family books or charts, engravings on rings, family portraits, engravings on urns, crypts, or tombstones, and the like, is not made inadmissible by the hearsay rule when offered to prove the birth, marriage, divorce, death, parent and child relationship, race, ancestry, relationship by blood or marriage, or other similar fact of the family history of a member of the family by blood or marriage.
(15) Statements in documents affecting an interest in property. A statement contained in a document purporting to establish or affect an interest in property if the matter stated was relevant to the purpose of the document, unless dealings with the property since the document was	**C.E.C. § 1330. Recitals in writings affecting property** Evidence of a statement contained in a deed of conveyance or a will or other writing purporting to affect an interest in real or personal property is not made inadmissible by the hearsay rule if: (a) The matter stated was relevant to the

110

made have been inconsistent with the truth of the statement or the purport of the document.	purpose of the writing; (b) The matter stated would be relevant to an issue as to an interest in the property; and (c) The dealings with the property since the statement was made have not been inconsistent with the truth of the statement.

4. *Statements in Ancient Documents (Rule 803(16))*

Fed. R. Evid. 803. Hearsay Exceptions; Availability of Declarant Immaterial The following are not excluded by the hearsay rule, even though the declarant is available as a witness: **(16) Statements in ancient documents.** Statements in a document in existence twenty years or more the authenticity of which is established.	**C.E.C. 1331. Recitals in ancient writings** Evidence of a statement is not made inadmissible by the hearsay rule if the statement is contained in a writing more than 30 years old and the statement has been since generally acted upon as true by persons having an interest in the matter.

5. Market Reports and Commercial Publications (Rule 803(17))

Fed. R. Evid. 803. Hearsay Exceptions; Availability of Declarant Immaterial The following are not excluded by the hearsay rule, even though the declarant is available as a witness: **(17) Market reports, commercial publications.** Market quotations, tabulations, lists, directories, or other published compilations, generally used and relied upon by the public or by persons in particular occupations.	**C.E.C. § 1340. Publications relied upon as accurate in the course of business** Evidence of a statement, other than an opinion, contained in a tabulation, list, directory, register, or other published compilation is not made inadmissible by the hearsay rule if the compilation is generally used and relied upon as accurate in the course of a business as defined in Section 1270.

6. Learned Treatises (Rule 803(18))

Fed. R. Evid. 803. Hearsay Exceptions; Availability of Declarant Immaterial The following are not excluded by the hearsay rule, even though the declarant is available as a witness: **(18) Learned treatises.** To the extent called to the attention of an expert witness upon cross-examination or relied upon by the expert witness in direct examination, statements contained in published treatises, periodicals, or pamphlets on a subject of history, medicine, or other science or art, established as a reliable authority by the testimony or admission of the witness or by other expert testimony or by judicial notice. If admitted, the statements may be read into evidence but may not be received as exhibits.	**C.E.C. § 1341. Publications concerning facts of general notoriety and interests** Historical works, books of science or art, and published maps or charts, made by persons indifferent between the parties, are not made inadmissible by the hearsay rule when offered to prove facts of general notoriety and interest.

7. *Reputation (Rules 803(19), 803(20), and 803(21))*

Fed. R. Evid. 803. Hearsay Exceptions; Availability of Declarant Immaterial

The following are not excluded by the hearsay rule, even though the declarant is available as a witness:

(19) Reputation concerning personal or family history. Reputation among members of a person's family by blood, adoption, or marriage, or among a person's associates, or in the community, concerning a person's birth, adoption, marriage, divorce, death, legitimacy, relationship by blood, adoption, or marriage, ancestry, or other similar fact of personal or family history.

C.E.C. § 1313. Reputation in family concerning family history

Evidence of reputation among members of a family is not made inadmissible by the hearsay rule if the reputation concerns the birth, marriage, divorce, death, parent and child relationship, race, ancestry, relationship by blood or marriage, or other similar fact of the family history of a member of the family by blood or marriage.

C.E.C. § 1314. Reputation in community concerning family history

Evidence of reputation in a community concerning the date or fact of birth, marriage, divorce, or death of a person resident in the community at the time of the reputation is not made inadmissible by the hearsay rule.

(20) Reputation concerning boundaries or general history. Reputation in a community, arising before the controversy, as to boundaries of or customs affecting lands in the community, and reputation as to events of general history important to the community or State or nation in which located.

C.E.C. § 1320. Reputation concerning community history

Evidence of reputation in a community is not made inadmissible by the hearsay rule if the reputation concerns an event of general history of the community or of the state or nation of which the community is a part and the event was of importance to the community.

C.E.C. § 1321. Reputation concerning public interest in property

Evidence of reputation in a community is not made inadmissible by the hearsay rule if the reputation concerns the interest of the public in property in the community and the reputation arose before controversy.

113

	C.E.C. § 1322. Reputation concerning boundary or custom affecting land Evidence of reputation in a community is not made inadmissible by the hearsay rule if the reputation concerns boundaries of, or customs affecting, land in the community and the reputation arose before controversy. C.E.C. § 1323. Statement concerning boundary Evidence of a statement concerning the boundary of land is not made inadmissible by the hearsay rule if the declarant is unavailable as a witness and had sufficient knowledge of the subject, but evidence of a statement is not admissible under this section if the statement was made under circumstances such as to indicate its lack of trustworthiness.
(21) Reputation as to character. Reputation of a person's character among associates or in the community.	**C.E.C. § 1324. Reputation concerning character** Evidence of a person's general reputation with reference to his character or a trait of his character at a relevant time in the community in which he then resided or in a group with which he then habitually associated is not made inadmissible by the hearsay rule.

8. *Judgment of Previous Conviction (Rule 803(22)) and Concerning Personal, Family, or General History, or Boundaries (Rule 803(23))*

Fed. R. Evid. 803. Hearsay Exceptions; Availability of Declarant Immaterial The following are not excluded by the hearsay rule, even though the declarant is available as a witness: **(22) Judgment of previous conviction.** Evidence of a final judgment, entered after	**C.E.C. § 1300. Judgment of conviction of crime punishable as felony** Evidence of a final judgment adjudging a

114

a trial or upon a plea of guilty (but not upon a plea of nolo contendere), adjudging a person guilty of a crime punishable by death or imprisonment in excess of one year, to prove any fact essential to sustain the judgment, but not including, when offered by the Government in a criminal prosecution for purposes other than impeachment, judgments against persons other than the accused. The pendency of an appeal may be shown but does not affect admissibility.

person guilty of a crime punishable as a felony is not made inadmissible by the hearsay rule when offered in a civil action to prove any fact essential to the judgment whether or not the judgment was based on a plea of nolo contendere.

C.E.C. § 1301. Judgment against person entitled to indemnity
Evidence of a final judgment is not made inadmissible by the hearsay rule when offered by the judgment debtor to prove any fact which was essential to the judgment in an action in which he seeks to:
(a) Recover partial or total indemnity or exoneration for money paid or liability incurred because of the judgment;
(b) Enforce a warranty to protect the judgment debtor against the liability determined by the judgment; or
(c) Recover damages for breach of warranty substantially the same as the warranty determined by the judgment to have been breached.

C.E.C. § 1302. Judgment determining liability of third person
When the liability, obligation, or duty of a third person is in issue in a civil action, evidence of a final judgment against that person is not made inadmissible by the hearsay rule when offered to prove such liability, obligation, or duty.

(23) Judgment as to personal, family, or general history, or boundaries.
Judgments as proof of matters of personal, family or general history, or boundaries, essential to the judgment, if the same would be provable by evidence of reputation.

CHAPTER
4

Evidence of Character, Uncharged Misconduct, and Similar Events

B.   CHARACTER EVIDENCE

Fed. R. Evid. 404. Character Evidence Not Admissible to Prove Conduct; Exceptions; Other Crimes

(a) Character evidence generally. Evidence of a person's character or a trait of character is not admissible for the purpose of proving action in conformity therewith on a particular occasion, except:

C.E.C. § 1101. Evidence of character to prove conduct
(a) Except as provided in this section and in Sections 1102, 1103, 1108, and 1109, evidence of a person's character or a trait of his or her character (whether in the form of an opinion, evidence of reputation, or evidence of specific instances of his or her conduct) is inadmissible when offered to prove his or her conduct on a specified occasion.

C.E.C. § 1104. Character trait for care or skill
Except as provided in Sections 1102 and 1103, evidence of a trait of a person's character with respect to care or skill is inadmissible to prove the quality of his conduct on a specified occasion.

C.E.C. § 1102. Opinion and reputation evidence of character of criminal defendant to prove conduct
In a criminal action, evidence of the defendant's character or a trait of his character in the form of an opinion or evidence of his reputation is not made inadmissible by Section 1101 if such evidence is:

(1) Character of accused. In a criminal case, evidence of a pertinent trait of character offered by an accused, or by the prosecution to rebut the same, ...

	(a) Offered by the defendant to prove his conduct in conformity with such character or trait of character. (b) Offered by the prosecution to rebut evidence adduced by the defendant under subdivision (a). **C.E.C. § 1103. ... evidence of defendant's character or trait for violence...** (b) In a criminal action, evidence of the defendant's character for violence or trait of character for violence (in the form of an opinion, evidence of reputation, or evidence of specific instances of conduct) is not made inadmissible by Section 1101 if the evidence is offered by the prosecution to prove conduct of the defendant in conformity with the character or trait of character and is offered after evidence that the victim had a character for violence or a trait of character tending to show violence has been adduced by the defendant under paragraph (1) of subdivision (a).
...or if evidence of a trait of character of the alleged victim of the crime is offered by an accused and admitted under Rule 404(a)(2), evidence of the same trait of character of the accused offered by the prosecution;	
(2) Character of Alleged Victim.—In a criminal case, and subject to the limitations imposed by Rule 412, evidence of a pertinent trait of character of the alleged victim of the crime offered by an accused, or by the prosecution to rebut the same, or evidence of a character trait of peacefulness of the alleged victim offered by the prosecution in a homicide case to rebut evidence that the alleged victim was the first aggressor;	**C.E.C. § 1103. Character evidence of crime victim to prove conduct; evidence of defendant's character or trait for violence; evidence of manner of dress of victim; evidence of complaining witness' sexual conduct** (a) In a criminal action, evidence of the character or a trait of character (in the form of an opinion, evidence of reputation, or evidence of specific instances of conduct) of the victim of the crime for which the defendant is being prosecuted is not made inadmissible by Section 1101 if the evidence is: (1) Offered by the defendant to prove conduct of the victim in conformity with the character or trait of character. (2) Offered by the prosecution to rebut evidence adduced by the defendant under paragraph (1).

3) Character of witness. Evidence of the character of a witness, as provided in rules 607, 608, and 609.

(b) Other crimes, wrongs, or acts. Evidence of other crimes, wrongs, or acts is not admissible to prove the character of a person in order to show action in conformity therewith. It may, however, be admissible for other purposes, such as proof of motive, opportunity, intent, preparation, plan, knowledge, identity, or absence of mistake or accident, provided that upon request by the accused, the prosecution in a criminal case shall provide reasonable notice in advance of trial, or during trial if the court excuses pretrial notice on good cause shown, of the general nature of any such evidence it intends to introduce at trial.

Fed. R. Evid. 405. Methods of Proving Character
(a) Reputation or opinion. In all cases in which evidence of character or a trait of character of a person is admissible, proof may be made by testimony as to reputation or by testimony in the form of an opinion. On cross-examination, inquiry is allowable into relevant specific instances of conduct.
(b) Specific instances of conduct. In cases in which character or a trait of character of a person is an essential element of a charge, claim, or defense, proof may also be made of specific instances of that person's conduct.

C.E.C. § 1101. Evidence of character to prove conduct
(c) Nothing in this section affects the admissibility of evidence offered to support or attack the credibility of a witness.

C.E.C. § 1101. Evidence of character to prove conduct
(b) Nothing in this section prohibits the admission of evidence that a person committed a crime, civil wrong, or other act when relevant to prove some fact (such as motive, opportunity, intent, preparation, plan, knowledge, identity, absence of mistake or accident, or whether a defendant in a prosecution for an unlawful sexual act or attempted unlawful sexual act did not reasonably and in good faith believe that the victim consented) other than his or her disposition to commit such an act.

C.E.C. § 1100. Manner of proof of character
Except as otherwise provided by statute, any otherwise admissible evidence (including evidence in the form of an opinion, evidence of reputation, and evidence of specific instances of such person's conduct) is admissible to prove a person's character or a trait of his character.

2. *Character Evidence Offered for Non-Credibility Purposes*

e. Proving Character as Circumstantial Evidence of Out-of-Court Conduct

ii. *Evidence of a Criminal Defendant's Character*

(a) In General

Questions for Classroom Discussion
Casebook page 334

1. [The following is based on question 6 from page 334 of the casebook.] Prosecution of Defendant for the murder of Victim. The prosecution alleges that Defendant planned and carried out the murder of Victim, Defendant's business rival. To prove Defendant committed the crime, the prosecution calls Witness during its case-in-chief to testify that she has known Defendant for many years, and that in her opinion, Defendant is a violent person. Defendant objects. How should the court rule under the federal rules of evidence? The C.E.C.?

2. [The following is based on question 7 from page 334 of the casebook.] Same case. During his case-in-chief, Defendant calls Witness to testify that she has lived in the same community as Defendant for many years, she knows Defendant's reputation for peacefulness, and Defendant's reputation is that he is a peaceful person. The prosecution objects that the defendant has offered inadmissible character evidence. How should the court rule under the Federal Rules? The C.E.C.?

3. Same case. On cross-examination of Defendant's witness, the prosecutor asks, "Did you know that when he was in law school Defendant beat up his Evidence professor?" How should the court rule under the Federal Rules? The C.E.C.?

(b) Sexual Assault and Child Molestation Cases

Fed. R. Evid. 413. Evidence of Similar Crimes in Sexual Assault Cases	C.E.C. § 1108. Evidence of another sexual offense by defendant; disclosure; construction of section
(a) In a criminal case in which the defendant is accused of an offense of sexual assault, evidence of the defendant's commission of another offense or offenses of sexual assault is admissible, and may be considered for its bearing on any matter to which it is relevant.	(a) In a criminal action in which the defendant is accused of a sexual offense, evidence of the defendant's commission of another sexual offense or offenses is not made inadmissible by Section 1101, if the evidence is not inadmissible pursuant to

(b) In a case in which the Government intends to offer evidence under this rule, the attorney for the Government shall disclose the evidence to the defendant, including statements of witnesses or a summary of the substance of any testimony that is expected to be offered, at least fifteen days before the scheduled date of trial or at such later time as the court may allow for good cause. (c) This rule shall not be construed to limit the admission or consideration of evidence under any other rule. (d) For purposes of this rule and Rule 415, "offense of sexual assault" means a crime under Federal law or the law of a State (as defined in section 513 of title 18, United States Code) that involved--(1) any conduct proscribed by chapter 109A of title 18, United States Code; (2) contact, without consent, between any part of the defendant's body or an object and the genitals or anus of another person; (3) contact, without consent, between the genitals or anus of the defendant and any part of another person's body; (4) deriving sexual pleasure or gratification from the infliction of death, bodily injury, or physical pain on another person; or (5) an attempt or conspiracy to engage in conduct described in paragraphs (1)-(4).	Section 352. (b) In an action in which evidence is to be offered under this section, the people shall disclose the evidence to the defendant, including statements of witnesses or a summary of the substance of any testimony that is expected to be offered in compliance with the provisions of Section 1054.7 of the Penal Code. (c) This section shall not be construed to limit the admission or consideration of evidence under any other section of this code. (d) As used in this section, the following definitions shall apply: (1) "Sexual offense" means a crime under the law of a state or of the United States that involved any of the following: (A) Any conduct proscribed by Section 243.4, 261, 261.5, 262, 264.1, 266c, 269, 286, 288, 288a, 288.2, 288.5, or 289, or subdivision (b), (c), or (d) of Section 311.2 or Section 311.3, 311.4, 311.10, 311.11, 314, or 647.6, of the Penal Code. (B) Any conduct proscribed by Section 220 of the Penal Code, except assault with intent to commit mayhem. (C) Contact, without consent, between any part of the defendant's body or an object and the genitals or anus of another person. (D) Contact, without consent, between the genitals or anus of the defendant and any part of another person's body. (E) Deriving sexual pleasure or gratification from the infliction of death, bodily injury, or physical pain on another person. (F) An attempt or conspiracy to engage in conduct described in this paragraph. (2) "Consent" shall have the same meaning as provided in Section 261.6 of the Penal Code, except that it does not include consent which is legally ineffective because of the age, mental disorder, or developmental or physical disability of the victim.

Fed. R. Evid. 414. Evidence of Similar Crimes in Child Molestation Cases

(a) In a criminal case in which the defendant is accused of an offense of child molestation, evidence of the defendant's commission of another offense or offenses of child molestation is admissible, and may be considered for its bearing on any matter to which it is relevant.

(b) In a case in which the Government intends to offer evidence under this rule, the attorney for the Government shall disclose the evidence to the defendant, including statements of witnesses or a summary of the substance of any testimony that is expected to be offered, at least fifteen days before the scheduled date of trial or at such later time as the court may allow for good cause.

(c) This rule shall not be construed to limit the admission or consideration of evidence under any other rule.

Fed. R. Evid. 415. Evidence of Similar Acts in Civil Cases Concerning Sexual Assault or Child Molestation.

(a) In a civil case in which a claim for damages or other relief is predicated on a party's alleged commission of conduct constituting an offense of sexual assault or child molestation, evidence of that party's commission of another offense or offenses of sexual assault or child molestation is admissible and may be considered as provided in Rule 413 and Rule 414 of these rules.

(b) A party who intends to offer evidence under this Rule shall disclose the evidence to the party against whom it will be offered, including statements of witnesses or a summary of the substance of any testimony that is expected to be offered, at least fifteen days before the scheduled date of trial or at such later time as the court may allow for good cause.

(c) This rule shall not be construed to limit the admission or consideration of evidence under any other rule.

C.E.C. § 1109. Evidence of defendant's other acts of domestic violence
(a)(1) Except as provided in subdivision (e) or (f), in a criminal action in which the defendant is accused of an offense involving domestic violence, evidence of the defendant's commission of other domestic violence is not made inadmissible by Section 1101 if the evidence is not inadmissible pursuant to Section 352.
(2) Except as provided in subdivision (e) or (f), in a criminal action in which the defendant is accused of an offense involving abuse of an elder or dependent person, evidence of the defendant's commission of other abuse of an elder or dependent person is not made inadmissible by Section 1101 if the evidence is not inadmissible pursuant to Section 352.
(b) In an action in which evidence is to be offered under this section, the people shall disclose the evidence to the defendant, including statements of witnesses or a summary of the substance of any testimony that is expected to be offered, in compliance with the provisions of Section 1054.7 of the Penal Code.
(c) This section shall not be construed to limit or preclude the admission or consideration of evidence under any other statute or case law.
(d) As used in this section, "domestic violence" has the meaning set forth in Section 13700 of the Penal Code. "Abuse of an elder or a dependent person" means physical or sexual abuse, neglect, financial abuse, abandonment, isolation, abduction, or other treatment that results in physical harm, pain, or mental suffering, the deprivation of care by a caregiver, or other deprivation by a custodian or provider of goods or services that are necessary to avoid physical harm or mental suffering.

	Subject to a hearing conducted pursuant to Section 352, which shall include consideration of any corroboration and remoteness in time, "domestic violence" has the further meaning as set forth in Section 6211 of the Family Code if the act occurred no more than five years before the charged offense. (e) Evidence of acts occurring more than 10 years before the charged offense is inadmissible under this section, unless the court determines that the admission of this evidence is in the interest of justice. (f) Evidence of the findings and determinations of administrative agencies regulating the conduct of health facilities licensed under Section 1250 of the Health and Safety Code is inadmissible under this section.

Questions for Classroom Discussion
Casebook Page 336

1. [The following is based on question 16 from page 336 of the casebook.] Prosecution of Defendant for rape of Victim, who was attacked while walking to her car after seeing a movie. Defendant denies being the perpetrator. To prove that Defendant committed the crime, the prosecution calls during its case-in-chief Witness to testify that Defendant has committed several rapes in the past few years. Defendant objects. How should the court rule under the Federal Rules? The C.E.C.?

2. [The following is based on question 17 from page 336 of the casebook.] Same case as in Question 1. The prosecution also wishes to offer evidence that Defendant has a community reputation as a dangerous sex criminal. Defendant objects. How should the court rule under the Federal Rules? The C.E.C.?

3. [The following is based on question 18 from page 336 of the casebook.] Same case as in Question 1. The prosecution wishes to offer evidence that Defendant has committed two acts of child molestation. Defendant objects. How should the court rule under the Federal Rules? The C.E.C.?

4. Civil action for assault. Plaintiff alleges Defendant sexually assaulted her. Plaintiff offers evidence that Defendant committed other acts of sexual assault. Defendant objects. How should the court rule under the Federal Rules? The C.E.C.?

5. Criminal prosecution for assault. Defendant allegedly beat his wife. Prosecution offers evidence that Defendant beat his wife on previous occasions. Defendant objects. How should the court rule under the Federal Rules? The C.E.C.?

iii. *Evidence of an Alleged Crime Victim's Character*

(a) **Defendant's Proof of an Alleged Crime Victim's Character**

Fed. R. Evid. 404. Character Evidence Not Admissible to Prove Conduct; Exceptions; Other Crimes	C.E.C. § 1103. Character evidence of crime victim to prove conduct; evidence of defendant's character or trait for violence; evidence of manner of dress of victim; evidence of complaining witness' sexual conduct
... **(2) Character of alleged victim.** Evidence of a pertinent trait of character of the alleged victim of the crime offered by an accused, or by the prosecution to rebut the same, or evidence of a character trait of peacefulness of the alleged victim offered by the prosecution in a homicide case to rebut evidence that the alleged victim was the first aggressor;	(a) In a criminal action, evidence of the character or a trait of character (in the form of an opinion, evidence of reputation, or evidence of specific instances of conduct) of the victim of the crime for which the defendant is being prosecuted is not made inadmissible by Section 1101 if the evidence is: (1) Offered by the defendant to prove conduct of the victim in conformity with the character or trait of character. (2) Offered by the prosecution to rebut evidence adduced by the defendant under paragraph (1).

1. Murder prosecution. Defendant testifies he acted in self defense after victim attacked him. The prosecution offers the testimony of victim's sister, who says victim had a reputation for peacefulness. Defendant objects. How should the court rule under the Federal Rules? The C.E.C.?

2. Same case. Defendant offers the direct examination testimony of victim's neighbor that he once saw the victim assault his Evidence professor. The prosecution objects. How should the court rule under the Federal Rules? The C.E.C.?

(b)   Special Rule for Rape Victims

Fed. R. Evid. 412. Sex Offense Cases; Relevance of Alleged Victim's Past Sexual Behavior or Alleged Sexual Predisposition	C.E.C. § 1103. Character evidence of crime victim to prove conduct; evidence of defendant's character or trait for violence; evidence of manner of dress of victim; evidence of complaining witness' sexual conduct
(a) Evidence generally inadmissible.—The following evidence is not admissible in any civil or criminal proceeding involving alleged sexual misconduct except as provided in subdivisions (b) and (c): (1) Evidence offered to prove that any alleged victim engaged in other sexual behavior. (2) Evidence offered to prove any alleged victim's sexual predisposition. (b) Exceptions.— (1) In a criminal case, the following evidence is admissible, if otherwise admissible under these rules: (A) evidence of specific instances of sexual behavior by the alleged victim offered to prove that a person other than the accused was the source of semen, injury or other physical evidence; (B) evidence of specific instances of sexual behavior by the alleged victim with respect to the person accused of the sexual misconduct offered by the accused to prove consent or by the prosecution; and (C) evidence the exclusion of which would violate the constitutional rights of the defendant. (2) In a civil case, evidence offered to prove the sexual behavior or sexual predisposition of any alleged victim is admissible if it is otherwise admissible under these rules and its probative value substantially outweighs the danger of harm to any victim and of unfair prejudice to any party. Evidence of an alleged victim's reputation is admissible only if it has been placed in controversy by the alleged victim. (c) Procedure to determine admissibility.— (1) A party intending to offer evidence under subdivision (b) must-	(c)(1) Notwithstanding any other provision of this code to the contrary, and except as provided in this subdivision, in any prosecution under Section 261, 262, or 264.1 of the Penal Code, or under Section 286, 288a, or 289 of the Penal Code, or for assault with intent to commit, attempt to commit, or conspiracy to commit a crime defined in any of those sections, except where the crime is alleged to have occurred in a local detention facility, as defined in Section 6031.4, or in a state prison, as defined in Section 4504, opinion evidence, reputation evidence, and evidence of specific instances of the complaining witness' sexual conduct, or any of that evidence, is not admissible by the defendant in order to prove consent by the complaining witness. (2) Notwithstanding paragraph (3), evidence of the manner in which the victim was dressed at the time of the commission of the offense shall not be admissible when offered by either party on the issue of consent in any prosecution for an offense specified in paragraph (1), unless the evidence is determined by the court to be relevant and admissible in the interests of justice. The proponent of the evidence shall make an offer of proof outside the hearing of the jury. The court shall then make its determination and at that time, state the reasons for its ruling on the record. For the purposes of this paragraph, "manner of dress" does not include the condition of the victim's clothing before, during, or after the commission of the offense. (3) Paragraph (1) shall not be applicable to

(A) file a written motion at least 14 days before trial specifically describing the evidence and stating the purpose for which it is offered unless the court, for good cause requires a different time for filing or permits filing during trial; and

(B) serve the motion on all parties and notify the alleged victim or, when appropriate, the alleged victim's guardian or representative.

(2) Before admitting evidence under this rule the court must conduct a hearing in camera and afford the victim and parties a right to attend and be heard. The motion, related papers, and the record of the hearing must be sealed and remain under seal unless the court orders otherwise.

evidence of the complaining witness' sexual conduct with the defendant.

(4) If the prosecutor introduces evidence, including testimony of a witness, or the complaining witness as a witness gives testimony, and that evidence or testimony relates to the complaining witness' sexual conduct, the defendant may cross-examine the witness who gives the testimony and offer relevant evidence limited specifically to the rebuttal of the evidence introduced by the prosecutor or given by the complaining witness.

(5) Nothing in this subdivision shall be construed to make inadmissible any evidence offered to attack the credibility of the complaining witness as provided in Section 782.

(6) As used in this section, "complaining witness" means the alleged victim of the crime charged, the prosecution of which is subject to this subdivision.

C.E.C. § 1106. Sexual harassment, sexual assault, or sexual battery cases; opinion or reputation evidence of plaintiff's sexual conduct; inadmissibility; exception; cross-examination

(a) In any civil action alleging conduct which constitutes sexual harassment, sexual assault, or sexual battery, opinion evidence, reputation evidence, and evidence of specific instances of plaintiff's sexual conduct, or any of such evidence, is not admissible by the defendant in order to prove consent by the plaintiff or the absence of injury to the plaintiff, unless the injury alleged by the plaintiff is in the nature of loss of consortium.

(b) Subdivision (a) shall not be applicable to evidence of the plaintiff's sexual conduct with the alleged perpetrator.

(c) If the plaintiff introduces evidence, including testimony of a witness, or the plaintiff as a witness gives testimony, and the evidence or testimony relates to the plaintiff's sexual conduct, the defendant may cross-examine the witness who gives the testimony and offer relevant evidence limited specifically to the rebuttal of the evidence introduced by the plaintiff or given by the plaintiff.

(d) Nothing in this section shall be construed to make inadmissible any evidence offered to attack the credibility of the plaintiff as provided in Section 783.

Question for Classroom Discussion
Casebook Page 341

Civil action for assault. Plaintiff claims defendant raped her. Defendant, a professional basketball player, claims he and plaintiff engaged in consensual sex. There were no other witnesses to the encounter between plaintiff and defendant and the physical evidence is inconclusive on the question of consent. On direct examination, plaintiff said nothing about her sexual conduct with others. Defendant offers evidence that plaintiff engaged in consensual sex with other members of the same basketball team on the night in question. Plaintiff objects. How should the court rule under the Federal Rules? The C.E.C.?

C. OTHER CRIMES, WRONGS, OR ACTS

Fed. R. Evid. 404(b). Other crimes, wrongs, or acts.	**C.E.C. § 1101. Evidence of character to prove conduct**
Evidence of other crimes, wrongs, or acts is not admissible to prove the character of a person in order to show action in conformity therewith. It may, however, be admissible for other purposes, such as proof of motive, opportunity, intent, preparation, plan, knowledge, identity, or absence of mistake or accident, provided that upon request by the accused, the prosecution in a criminal case shall provide reasonable notice in advance of trial, or during trial if the court excuses pretrial notice on good cause shown, of the general nature of any such evidence it intends to introduce at trial.	(b) Nothing in this section prohibits the admission of evidence that a person committed a crime, civil wrong, or other act when relevant to prove some fact (such as motive, opportunity, intent, preparation, plan, knowledge, identity, absence of mistake or accident, or whether a defendant in a prosecution for an unlawful sexual act or attempted unlawful sexual act did not reasonably and in good faith believe that the victim consented) other than his or her disposition to commit such an act.

D.   HABIT EVIDENCE

Fed. R. Evid. 406. Habit; Routine Practice	C.E.C. § 1105. Habit or custom to prove specific behavior
Evidence of the habit of a person or of the routine practice of an organization, whether corroborated or not and regardless of the presence of eyewitnesses, is relevant to prove that the conduct of the person or organization on a particular occasion was in conformity with the habit or routine practice.	Any otherwise admissible evidence of habit or custom is admissible to prove conduct on a specified occasion in conformity with the habit or custom.

CHAPTER
5

Exclusion of Other Relevant Evidence
for Reasons of Policy

B.   SUBSEQUENT REMEDIAL MEASURES

Fed. R. Evid. 407. Subsequent Remedial Measures	C.E.C. § 1151. Subsequent remedial conduct
When, after an injury or harm allegedly caused by an event, measure are taken that, if taken previously, would have made the injury or harm less likely to occur, evidence of the subsequent measures is not admissible to prove negligence, culpable conduct, a defect in a product, a defect in a product's design, or a need for a warning or instruction. This rule does not require the exclusion of evidence of subsequent measures when offered for another purpose, such as proving ownership, control, or feasibility of precautionary measures, if controverted, or impeachment.	When, after the occurrence of an event, remedial or precautionary measures are taken, which, if taken previously, would have tended to make the event less likely to occur, evidence of such subsequent measures is inadmissible to prove negligence or culpable conduct in connection with the event.

Question for Classroom Discussion
Casebook Page 389

Products liability action seeking to hold defendant, manufacturer of an intrauterine birth control device, strictly liable for manufacturing an allegedly defective product that injured plaintiff. Plaintiff offers evidence that, after many doctors reported that patients using the device were rendered sterile, defendant altered the design of the device. Defendant objects. How should the court rule under the Federal Rules? The C.E.C.?

C. COMPROMISE AND PAYMENT OF MEDICAL AND SIMILAR EXPENSES

Fed. R. Evid. 408. Compromise and Offers to Compromise
(a) Prohibited uses.—Evidence of the following is not admissible on behalf of any party, when offered to prove liability for, invalidity of, or amount of a claim that was disputed as to validity or amount, or to impeach through a prior inconsistent statement or contradiction:
(1) furnishing or offering or promising to furnish—or accepting or offering or promising to accept—a valuable consideration in compromising or attempting to compromise the claim; and
(2) conduct or statements made in compromise negotiations regarding the claim, except when offered in a criminal case and the negotiations related to a claim by a public office or agency in the exercise of regulatory, investigative, or enforcement authority.
(b) Permitted uses.—This rule does not require exclusion if the evidence is offered for purposes not prohibited by subdivision (a). Examples of permissible purposes include proving a witness's bias or prejudice; negating a contention of undue delay; and proving an effort to obstruct a criminal investigation or prosecution.

Fed. R. Evid. 409. Payment of Medical and Similar Expenses
Evidence of furnishing or offering or promising to pay medical, hospital, or similar expenses occasioned by an injury is not admissible to prove liability for the injury.

C.E.C. § 1152. Offers to compromise
(a) Evidence that a person has, in compromise or from humanitarian motives, furnished or offered or promised to furnish money or any other thing, act, or service to another who has sustained or will sustain or claims that he or she has sustained or will sustain loss or damage, as well as any conduct or statements made in negotiation thereof, is inadmissible to prove his or her liability for the loss or damage or any part of it.
(b) In the event that evidence of an offer to compromise is admitted in an action for breach of the covenant of good faith and fair dealing or violation of subdivision (h) of Section 790.03 of the Insurance Code, then at the request of the party against whom the evidence is admitted, or at the request of the party who made the offer to compromise that was admitted, evidence relating to any other offer or counteroffer to compromise the same or substantially the same claimed loss or damage shall also be admissible for the same purpose as the initial evidence regarding settlement. Other than as may be admitted in an action for breach of the covenant of good faith and fair dealing or violation of subdivision (h) of Section 790.03 of the Insurance Code, evidence of settlement offers shall not be admitted in a motion for a new trial, in any proceeding involving an additur or remittitur, or on appeal.
(c) This section does not affect the admissibility of evidence of any of the following:
(1) Partial satisfaction of an asserted claim or demand without questioning its validity when such evidence is offered to prove the validity of the claim.
(2) A debtor's payment or promise to pay all or a part of his or her preexisting debt

when such evidence is offered to prove the creation of a new duty on his or her part or a revival of his or her preexisting duty.

C.E.C. § 1154. Offer to discount a claim
Evidence that a person has accepted or offered or promised to accept a sum of money or any other thing, act, or service in satisfaction of a claim, as well as any conduct or statements made in negotiation thereof, is inadmissible to prove the invalidity of the claim or any part of it.

C.E.C. § 1160. Admissibility of expressions of sympathy or benevolence; definitions
(a) The portion of statements, writings, or benevolent gestures expressing sympathy or a general sense of benevolence relating to the pain, suffering, or death of a person involved in an accident and made to that person or to the family of that person shall be inadmissible as evidence of an admission of liability in a civil action. A statement of fault, however, which is part of, or in addition to, any of the above shall not be inadmissible pursuant to this section.
(b) For purposes of this section:
(1) "Accident" means an occurrence resulting in injury or death to one or more persons which is not the result of willful action by a party.
(2) "Benevolent gestures" means actions which convey a sense of compassion or commiseration emanating from humane impulses.
(3) "Family" means the spouse, parent, grandparent, stepmother, stepfather, child, grandchild, brother, sister, half brother, half sister, adopted children of parent, or spouse's parents of an injured party.

Action for personal injuries suffered in an automobile accident. At the scene, defendant said to plaintiff, "You seem to be in a lot of pain. I am so sorry that I ran the red light." Defendant then followed plaintiff's ambulance to the hospital and paid plaintiff's hospital bill. After filing of the suit, defendant's lawyer offered to settle plaintiff's claim for $100,000. Plaintiff offers to testify to all these matters and defendant objects. How should the court rule under the Federal Rules? The C.E.C.?

D. PLEA EVIDENCE

Fed. R. Evid. 410. Inadmissibility of Pleas, Plea Discussions, and Related Statements	**C.E.C. § 1153. Offer to plead guilty or withdrawn plea of guilty by criminal defendant**
Except as otherwise provided in this rule, evidence of the following is not, in any civil or criminal proceeding, admissible against the defendant who made the plea or was a participant in the plea discussions: (1) a plea of guilty which was later withdrawn; (2) a plea of nolo contendere; (3) any statement made in the course of any proceedings under Rule 11 of the Federal Rules of Criminal Procedure or comparable state procedure regarding either of the foregoing pleas; or (4) any statement made in the course of plea discussions with an attorney for the prosecuting authority which do not result in a plea of guilty or which result in a plea of guilty later withdrawn. However, such a statement is admissible (i) in any proceeding wherein another statement made in	Evidence of a plea of guilty, later withdrawn, or of an offer to plead guilty to the crime charged or to any other crime, made by the defendant in a criminal action is inadmissible in any action or in any proceeding of any nature, including proceedings before agencies, commissions, boards, and tribunals. **C.E.C. § 1153.5. Offer for civil resolution of crimes against property** Evidence of an offer for civil resolution of a criminal matter pursuant to the provisions of Section 33 of the Code of Civil Procedure, or admissions made in the course of or negotiations for the offer shall not be admissible in any action.

the course of the same plea or plea discussions has been introduced and the statement ought in fairness be considered contemporaneously with it, or (ii) in a criminal proceeding for perjury or false statement if the statement was made by the defendant under oath, on the record and in the presence of counsel.

Question for Classroom Discussion
Casebook Page 408

Prosecution for murder. In a plea bargaining discussion between defense counsel and the prosector in the presence of defendant, the latter said, "You might as well take me to the gas chamber right now." No plea agreement was reached and the prosecution offered defendant's statement into evidence at trial to prove his consciousness of guilt. Is the statement admissible under the Federal Rules? The C.E.C.?

E. EVIDENCE OF LIABILITY INSURANCE

Fed. R. Evid. 411. Liability Insurance	**C.E.C. § 1155. Liability insurance**
Evidence that a person was or was not insured against liability is not admissible upon the issue whether the person acted negligently or otherwise wrongfully. This rule does not require the exclusion of evidence of insurance against liability when offered for another purpose, such as proof of agency, ownership, or control, or bias or prejudice of a witness.	Evidence that a person was, at the time a harm was suffered by another, insured wholly or partially against loss arising from liability for that harm is inadmissible to prove negligence or other wrongdoing.

CHAPTER
6

Examining Witnesses; Attacking and Supporting the Credibility of Witnesses

A.   MODE OF WITNESS EXAMINATION

Rule 611. Mode and Order of Interrogation and Presentation (a) Control by court. The court shall exercise reasonable control over the mode and order of interrogating witnesses and presenting evidence so as to (1) make the interrogation and presentation effective for the ascertainment of the truth, (2) avoid needless consumption of time, and (3) protect witnesses from harassment or undue embarrassment. (b) Scope of cross-examination. Cross-examination should be limited to the subject matter of the direct examination and matters affecting the credibility of the witness. The court may, in the exercise of discretion, permit inquiry into additional matters as if on direct examination. (c) Leading questions. Leading questions should not be used on the direct examination of a witness except as may be necessary to develop the witness' testimony. Ordinarily leading questions should be permitted on cross-examination. When a party calls a hostile witness, an adverse party, or a witness identified with an adverse party, interrogation may be by leading questions.	**C.E.C. § 320. Power of court to regulate order of proof** Except as otherwise provided by law, the court in its discretion shall regulate the order of proof. **C.E.C. § 765. Court to control mode of interrogation** (a) The court shall exercise reasonable control over the mode of interrogation of a witness so as to make interrogation as rapid, as distinct, and as effective for the ascertainment of the truth, as may be, and to protect the witness from undue harassment or embarrassment. (b) With a witness under the age of 14 or a dependent person with a substantial cognitive impairment, the court shall take special care to protect him or her from undue harassment or embarrassment, and to restrict the unnecessary repetition of questions. The court shall also take special care to ensure that questions are stated in a form which is appropriate to the age or cognitive level of the witness. The court may, in the interests of justice, on objection by a party, forbid the asking of a question which is in a form that is not reasonably likely to be understood by a person of the age or cognitive level of the witness.

C.E.C. § 760. Direct examination
"Direct examination" is the first examination of a witness upon a matter that is not within the scope of a previous examination of the witness.

C.E.C. § 761. Cross-examination
"Cross-examination" is the examination of a witness by a party other than the direct examiner upon a matter that is within the scope of the direct examination of the witness.

C.E.C. § 762. Redirect examination
"Redirect examination" is an examination of a witness by the direct examiner subsequent to the cross-examination of the witness.

C.E.C. § 763. Recross-examination
"Recross-examination" is an examination of a witness by a cross-examiner subsequent to a redirect examination of the witness.

C.E.C. § 764. Leading question
A "leading question" is a question that suggests to the witness the answer that the examining party desires.

C.E.C. § 773. Cross-examination
(a) A witness examined by one party may be cross-examined upon any matter within the scope of the direct examination by each other party to the action in such order as the court directs.
(b) The cross-examination of a witness by any party whose interest is not adverse to the party calling him is subject to the same rules that are applicable to the direct examination.

C.E.C. § 776. Examination of adverse party or person identified with adverse party

(a) A party to the record of any civil action, or a person identified with such a party, may be called and examined as if under cross-examination by any adverse party at any time during the presentation of evidence by the party calling the witness.

(b) A witness examined by a party under this section may be cross-examined by all other parties to the action in such order as the court directs; but, subject to subdivision (e), the witness may be examined only as if under redirect examination by:

(1) In the case of a witness who is a party, his own counsel and counsel for a party who is not adverse to the witness.

(2) In the case of a witness who is not a party, counsel for the party with whom the witness is identified and counsel for a party who is not adverse to the party with whom the witness is identified.

(c) For the purpose of this section, parties represented by the same counsel are deemed to be a single party.

(d) For the purpose of this section, a person is identified with a party if he is:

(1) A person for whose immediate benefit the action is prosecuted or defended by the party.

(2) A director, officer, superintendent, member, agent, employee, or managing agent of the party or of a person specified in paragraph (1), or any public employee of a public entity when such public entity is the party.

(3) A person who was in any of the relationships specified in paragraph (2) at the time of the act or omission giving rise to the cause of action.

(4) A person who was in any of the relationships specified in paragraph (2) at the time he obtained knowledge of the matter concerning which he is sought to be examined under this section.

	(e) Paragraph (2) of subdivision (b) does not require counsel for the party with whom the witness is identified and counsel for a party who is not adverse to the party with whom the witness is identified to examine the witness as if under redirect examination if the party who called the witness for examination under this section: (1) Is also a person identified with the same party with whom the witness is identified. (2) Is the personal representative, heir, successor, or assignee of a person identified with the same party with whom the witness is identified.

C.   WHO MAY IMPEACH

Fed. R. Evid. 607. Who May Impeach The credibility of a witness may be attacked by any party, including the party calling the witness.	**C.E.C. § 785. Parties may attack or support credibility** The credibility of a witness may be attacked or supported by any party, including the party calling him. **C.E.C. § 780. Testimony; proof of truthfulness; considerations** Except as otherwise provided by statute, the court or jury may consider in determining the credibility of a witness any matter that has any tendency in reason to prove or disprove the truthfulness of his testimony at the hearing, including but not limited to any of the following: (a) His demeanor while testifying and the manner in which he testifies. (b) The character of his testimony. (c) The extent of his capacity to perceive, to recollect, or to communicate any matter about which he testifies. (d) The extent of his opportunity to perceive any matter about which he testifies. (e) His character for honesty or veracity or their opposites.

	(f) The existence or nonexistence of a bias, interest, or other motive. (g) A statement previously made by him that is consistent with his testimony at the hearing. (h) A statement made by him that is inconsistent with any part of his testimony at the hearing. (i) The existence or nonexistence of any fact testified to by him. (j) His attitude toward the action in which he testifies or toward the giving of testimony. (k) His admission of untruthfulness.

E.   WITNESS CHARACTER

2.   *Reputation or Opinion Concerning Truthfulness*

Fed. R. Evid. 608. Evidence of Character and Conduct of Witness **(a) Opinion and reputation evidence of character.** The credibility of a witness may be attacked or supported by evidence in the form of opinion or reputation, but subject to these limitations: (1) the evidence may refer only to character for truthfulness or untruthfulness, and (2) evidence of truthful character is admissible only after the character of the witness for truthfulness has been attacked by opinion or reputation evidence or otherwise.	**C.E.C. § 786. Character evidence generally** Evidence of traits of his character other than honesty or veracity, or their opposites, is inadmissible to attack or support the credibility of a witness. **C.E.C. § 790. Good character of witness** Evidence of the good character of a witness is inadmissible to support his credibility unless evidence of his bad character has been admitted for the purpose of attacking his credibility.

3. *Conduct Probative of Truthfulness*

Fed. R. Evid. 608. Evidence of Character and Conduct of Witness

(b) Specific instances of conduct. Specific instances of the conduct of a witness, for the purpose of attacking or supporting the witness' character for truthfulness, other than conviction of crime as provided in Rule 609, may not be proved by extrinsic evidence. They may, however, in the discretion of the court, if probative of truthfulness or untruthfulness, be inquired into on cross-examination of the witness (1) concerning the witness' character for truthfulness or untruthfulness, or (2) concerning the character for truthfulness or untruthfulness of another witness as to which character the witness being cross-examined has testified. The giving of testimony, whether by an accused or by any other witness, does not operate as a waiver of the accused's or the witness' privilege against self-incrimination when examined with respect to matters which relate only to credibility.

C.E.C. § 787. Specific instances of conduct

Subject to Section 788, evidence of specific instances of his conduct relevant only as tending to prove a trait of his character is inadmissible to attack or support the credibility of a witness.

Cal. Const. Art. I, § 28(d). Right to Truth-in-Evidence
Except as provided by statute hereafter enacted by a two-thirds vote of the membership in each house of the Legislature, relevant evidence shall not be excluded in any criminal proceeding, including pretrial and post conviction motions and hearings, or in any trial or hearing of a juvenile for a criminal offense, whether heard in juvenile or adult court. Nothing in this section shall affect any existing statutory rule of evidence relating to privilege or hearsay, or Evidence Code, Sections 352, 782 or 1103. Nothing in this section shall affect any existing statutory or constitutional right of the press.

Questions for Classroom Discussion
Casebook Page 441

1. Civil action for wrongful death. Defendant calls a witness who testifies that, at the time plaintiff's decedent was shot, defendant was with witness eating dinner across town. On cross-examination, plaintiff asks, "Isn't it true that you lied on your law school application." Defendant objects. How should the court rule under the Federal Rules? The C.E.C.?

4. Conviction of crime

Fed. R. Evid. 609. Impeachment by Evidence of Conviction of Crime

(a) General rule.—For the purpose of attacking the character for truthfulness of a witness,

(1) evidence that a witness other than an accused has been convicted of a crime shall be admitted, subject to Rule 403, if the crime was punishable by death or imprisonment in excess of one year under the law under which the witness was convicted, and evidence that an accused has been convicted of such a crime shall be admitted if the court determines that the probative value of admitting this evidence outweighs its prejudicial effect to the accused; and

(2) evidence that any witness has been convicted of a crime shall be admitted regardless of the punishment, if it readily can be determined that establishing the elements of the crime required proof or admission of an act of dishonesty or false statement by the witness.

(b) Time limit. Evidence of a conviction under this rule is not admissible if a period of more than ten years has elapsed since the date of the conviction or of the release of the witness from the confinement imposed for that conviction, whichever is the later date, unless the court determines, in the interests of justice, that the probative value of the conviction supported by specific facts and circumstances substantially outweighs its prejudicial effect.

C.E.C. § 788. Prior felony conviction

For the purpose of attacking the credibility of a witness, it may be shown by the examination of the witness or by the record of the judgment that he has been convicted of a felony unless:

(a) A pardon based on his innocence has been granted to the witness by the jurisdiction in which he was convicted.

(b) A certificate of rehabilitation and pardon has been granted to the witness under the provisions of Chapter 3.5 (commencing with Section 4852.01) of Title 6 of Part 3 of the Penal Code.

(c) The accusatory pleading against the witness has been dismissed under the provisions of Penal Code Section 1203.4, but this exception does not apply to any criminal trial where the witness is being prosecuted for a subsequent offense.

(d) The conviction was under the laws of another jurisdiction and the witness has been relieved of the penalties and disabilities arising from the conviction pursuant to a procedure substantially equivalent to that referred to in subdivision (b) or (c).

Cal. Const. Art. I, § 28 (f) Use of Prior Convictions.

Any prior felony conviction of any person in any criminal proceeding, whether adult or juvenile, shall subsequently be used without limitation for purposes of impeachment or enhancement of sentence in any criminal proceeding. When a prior felony conviction is an element of any

However, evidence of a conviction more than 10 years old as calculated herein, is not admissible unless the proponent gives to the adverse party sufficient advance written notice of intent to use such evidence to provide the adverse party with a fair opportunity to contest the use of such evidence.

(c) Effect of pardon, annulment, or certificate of rehabilitation.
Evidence of a conviction is not admissible under this rule if (1) the conviction has been the subject of a pardon, annulment, certificate of rehabilitation, or other equivalent procedure based on a finding of the rehabilitation of the person convicted, and that person has not been convicted of a subsequent crime which was punishable by death or imprisonment in excess of one year, or (2) the conviction has been the subject of a pardon, annulment, or other equivalent procedure based on a finding of innocence.

(d) Juvenile adjudications.
Evidence of juvenile adjudications is generally not admissible under this rule. The court may, however, in a criminal case allow evidence of a juvenile adjudication of a witness other than the accused if conviction of the offense would be admissible to attack the credibility of an adult and the court is satisfied that admission in evidence is necessary for a fair determination of the issue of guilt or innocence.

(e) Pendency of appeal. The pendency of an appeal therefrom does not render evidence of a conviction inadmissible. Evidence of the pendency of an appeal is admissible.

felony offense, it shall be proven to the trier of fact in open court.

1. Prosecution for perjury. Defendant testifies in his own defense that he did not knowingly lie when he testified under oath. On cross-examination, the prosecutor asks, "Isn't it true that you were convicted last year of lying on your driver's license application, which is a misdemeanor? Defendant objects. How should the court rule under the Federal Rules? The C.E.C.?

2. Same case, except this time the prosecutor asks defendant, "Isn't it true that you were convicted of felony child molestation? Defendant objects. How should the court rule under the Federal Rules? The C.E.C.?

3. Same as preceding question, except defendant's child molestation conviction is twenty years old.

5.   *Religious Beliefs or Opinions*

Fed. R. Evid. 610. Religious Beliefs or Opinions	C.E.C. § 789. Religious belief
Evidence of the beliefs or opinions of a witness on matters of religion is not admissible for the purpose of showing that by reason of their nature the witness' credibility is impaired or enhanced.	Evidence of his religious belief or lack thereof is inadmissible to attack or support the credibility of a witness.

H.   PRIOR STATEMENTS OF WITNESSES

Fed. R. Evid. 801(d)(1). Definitions	
(d) Statements which are not hearsay. A statement is not hearsay if—	
(1) Prior statement by witness. The declarant testifies at the trial or hearing and is subject to cross-examination concerning the statement, and the statement is (A) inconsistent with the declarant's testimony, and was given under oath subject to the penalty of perjury at a trial, hearing, or	**C.E.C. § 1235. Inconsistent statements** Evidence of a statement made by a witness is not made inadmissible by the hearsay rule if the statement is inconsistent with his testimony at the hearing and is offered in compliance with Section 770.

other proceeding, or in a deposition, or (B) consistent with the declarant's testimony and is offered to rebut an express or implied charge against the declarant of recent fabrication or improper influence or motive,

Fed. R. Evid. 613. Prior Statements of Witnesses

a) Examining witness concerning prior statement. In examining a witness concerning a prior statement made by the witness, whether written or not, the statement need not be shown nor the contents disclosed to the witness at that time, but on request the same shall be shown or disclosed to opposing counsel.

(b) Extrinsic evidence of prior inconsistent statement of witness. Extrinsic evidence of a prior inconsistent statement by a witness is not admissible unless the witness is afforded an opportunity to explain or deny the same and the opposite party is afforded an opportunity to interrogate the witness thereon, or the interests of justice otherwise require. This provision does not apply to admissions of a party-opponent as defined in rule 801(d)(2).

C.E.C. § 1236. Prior consistent statements

Evidence of a statement previously made by a witness is not made inadmissible by the hearsay rule if the statement is consistent with his testimony at the hearing and is offered in compliance with Section 791.

C.E.C. § 768. Writings

(a) In examining a witness concerning a writing, it is not necessary to show, read, or disclose to him any part of the writing.

(b) If a writing is shown to a witness, all parties to the action must be given an opportunity to inspect it before any question concerning it may be asked of the witness.

C.E.C. § 769. Inconsistent statement or conduct

In examining a witness concerning a statement or other conduct by him that is inconsistent with any part of his testimony at the hearing, it is not necessary to disclose to him any information concerning the statement or other conduct.

C.E.C. § 770. Evidence of inconsistent statement of witness; exclusion; exceptions

Unless the interests of justice otherwise require, extrinsic evidence of a statement made by a witness that is inconsistent with any part of his testimony at the hearing shall be excluded unless:

(a) The witness was so examined while testifying as to give him an opportunity to explain or to deny the statement; or

(b) The witness has not been excused from giving further testimony in the action.

C.E.C. § 791. Prior consistent statement of witness

Evidence of a statement previously made by a witness that is consistent with his

	testimony at the hearing is inadmissible to support his credibility unless it is offered after: (a) Evidence of a statement made by him that is inconsistent with any part of his testimony at the hearing has been admitted for the purpose of attacking his credibility, and the statement was made before the alleged inconsistent statement; or (b) An express or implied charge has been made that his testimony at the hearing is recently fabricated or is influenced by bias or other improper motive, and the statement was made before the bias, motive for fabrication, or other improper motive is alleged to have arisen.

Questions for Classroom Discussion
Casebook page 483

1. Action for personal injuries suffered in an automobile accident. Plaintiff's witness testifies that defendant struck plaintiff in the crosswalk. On cross examination, defendant asks, "Didn't you tell the investigating police officer at the scene that plaintiff was jaywalking and was not in the crosswalk at the time of impact?" Plaintiff objects on the ground of hearsay. What result under the Federal Rules? The C.E.C.?

2. Same case. On cross examination, defendant asks, "Didn't plaintiff offer you $1,000 yesterday if you would testify that he was in the crosswalk? Plaintiff then offers the witness' deposition testimony, given months ago, in which he stated that plaintiff was in the crosswalk. Defendant objects on the ground of hearsay. What result under the Federal Rules? The C.E.C.?

CHAPTER
7

Lay and Expert Opinion Evidence

B.   LAY OPINION

Fed. R. Evid. 701. Opinion Testimony by Lay Witnesses	**C.E.C. § 800. Lay witnesses; opinion testimony**
If the witness is not testifying as an expert, the witness' testimony in the form of opinions or inferences is limited to those opinions or inferences which are (a) rationally based on the perception of the witness, (b) helpful to a clear understanding of the witness' testimony or the determination of a fact in issue, and (c) not based on scientific, technical, or other specialized knowledge within the scope of Rule 702.	If a witness is not testifying as an expert, his testimony in the form of an opinion is limited to such an opinion as is permitted by law, including but not limited to an opinion that is: (a) Rationally based on the perception of the witness; and (b) Helpful to a clear understanding of his testimony.

C.   EXPERT OPINION

Fed. R. Evid. 702. Testimony by Experts

If scientific, technical, or other specialized knowledge will assist the trier of fact to understand the evidence or to determine a fact in issue, a witness qualified as an expert by knowledge, skill, experience, training, or education, may testify thereto in the form of an opinion or otherwise, if (1) the testimony is based upon sufficient facts or data, (2) the testimony is the product of reliable principles and methods, and (3) the witness has applied the principles and methods reliably to the facts of the case.

C.E.C. § 801. Expert witnesses; opinion testimony

If a witness is testifying as an expert, his testimony in the form of an opinion is limited to such an opinion as is:
(a) Related to a subject that is sufficiently beyond common experience that the opinion of an expert would assist the trier of fact ….

C.E.C. § 720. Qualification as an expert witness

(a) A person is qualified to testify as an expert if he has special knowledge, skill, experience, training, or education sufficient to qualify him as an expert on the subject to which his testimony relates. Against the objection of a party, such special knowledge, skill, experience, training, or education must be shown before the witness may testify as an expert.
(b) A witness' special knowledge, skill, experience, training, or education may be shown by any otherwise admissible evidence, including his own testimony.

Question for Classroom Discussion
Casebook page 520

[The following is based on question 1 from page 520 of the casebook.] Murder prosecution. Defendant is an aging, bald, overweight law professor. A prosecution expert witness offers to testify that, based application of a radical new technology for DNA testing, the perpetrator's blood found at the crime scene reveals perpetrator had all these characteristics. While the validity of the test is not yet generally accepted among scientists, the test has been *published* in scientific journals, has a *low error rate,* the results are *subject to retesting,* and the test at least has *a reasonable level of acceptance* in the scientific community. Is the expert's opinion admissible under Rule 702? Under C.E.C. § 801?

8. *Expert Testimony Must Have a Proper Basis*

Fed. R. Evid. 703. Bases of Opinion Testimony by Experts	C.E.C. § 801. Expert witnesses; opinion testimony
The facts or data in the particular case upon which an expert bases an opinion or inference may be those perceived by or made known to the expert at or before the hearing. If of a type reasonably relied upon by experts in the particular field in forming opinions or inferences upon the subject, the facts or data need not be admissible in evidence in order for the opinion or inference to be admitted. Facts or data that are otherwise inadmissible shall not be disclosed to the jury by the proponent of the opinion or inference unless the court determines that their probative value in assisting the jury to evaluate the expert's opinion substantially outweighs their prejudicial effect.	If a witness is testifying as an expert, his testimony in the form of an opinion is limited to such an opinion as is: ... (b) Based on matter (including his special knowledge, skill, experience, training, and education) perceived by or personally known to the witness or made known to him at or before the hearing, whether or not admissible, that is of a type that reasonably may be relied upon by an expert in forming an opinion upon the subject to which his testimony relates, unless an expert is precluded by law from using such matter as a basis for his opinion. **C.E.C. § 803. Opinion based on improper matter** The court may, and upon objection shall, exclude testimony in the form of an opinion that is based in whole or in significant part on matter that is not a proper basis for such an opinion. In such case, the witness may, if there remains a proper basis for his opinion, then state his opinion after excluding from consideration the matter determined to be improper.

9. *Expert Testimony: Limits on Opinions Going to Ultimate Issues*

Fed. R. Evid. 704. Opinion on Ultimate Issue	C.E.C. § 805. Opinion on ultimate issue
(a) Except as provided in subdivision (b), testimony in the form of an opinion or inference otherwise admissible is not objectionable because it embraces an ultimate issue to be decided by the trier of fact.	Testimony in the form of an opinion that is otherwise admissible is not objectionable because it embraces the ultimate issue to be decided by the trier of fact.

(b) No expert witness testifying with respect to the mental state or condition of a defendant in a criminal case may state an opinion or inference as to whether the defendant did or did not have the mental state or condition constituting an element of the crime charged or of a defense thereto. Such ultimate issues are matters for the trier of fact alone.	**California Penal Code § 29. Mental state; restriction on expert testimony; determination by trier of fact** In the guilt phase of a criminal action, any expert testifying about a defendant's mental illness, mental disorder, or mental defect shall not testify as to whether the defendant had or did not have the required mental states, which include, but are not limited to, purpose, intent, knowledge, or malice aforethought, for the crimes charged. The question as to whether the defendant had or did not have the required mental states shall be decided by the trier of fact.
	C.E.C. § 870. Opinion as to sanity A witness may state his opinion as to the sanity of a person when: (a) The witness is an intimate acquaintance of the person whose sanity is in question; (b) The witness was a subscribing witness to a writing, the validity of which is in dispute, signed by the person whose sanity is in question and the opinion relates to the sanity of such person at the time the writing was signed; or (c) The witness is qualified under Section 800 or 801 to testify in the form of an opinion.

10. Expert Testimony: Disclosing Facts Underlying Opinion

Fed. R. Evid. 705. Disclosure of Facts or Data Underlying Expert Opinion The expert may testify in terms of opinion or inference and give reasons therefor without first testifying to the underlying facts or data, unless the court requires otherwise. The expert may in any event be required to disclose the underlying facts or data on cross-examination.	**C.E.C. § 802. Statement of basis of opinion** A witness testifying in the form of an opinion may state on direct examination the reasons for his opinion and the matter (including, in the case of an expert, his special knowledge, skill, experience, training, and education) upon which it is based, unless he is precluded by law from

using such reasons or matter as a basis for his opinion. The court in its discretion may require that a witness before testifying in the form of an opinion be first examined concerning the matter upon which his opinion is based.

C.E.C. § 721. Cross-examination of expert witness

(a) Subject to subdivision (b), a witness testifying as an expert may be cross-examined to the same extent as any other witness and, in addition, may be fully cross-examined as to (1) his or her qualifications, (2) the subject to which his or her expert testimony relates, and (3) the matter upon which his or her opinion is based and the reasons for his or her opinion.

(b) If a witness testifying as an expert testifies in the form of an opinion, he or she may not be cross-examined in regard to the content or tenor of any scientific, technical, or professional text, treatise, journal, or similar publication unless any of the following occurs:

(1) The witness referred to, considered, or relied upon such publication in arriving at or forming his or her opinion.

(2) The publication has been admitted in evidence.

(3) The publication has been established as a reliable authority by the testimony or admission of the witness or by other expert testimony or by judicial notice.

If admitted, relevant portions of the publication may be read into evidence but may not be received as exhibits.

Fed. R. Evid. 803. Hearsay Exceptions; Availability of Declarant Immaterial

The following are not excluded by the hearsay rule, even though the declarant is available as a witness:

(18) Learned treatises. To the extent called to the attention of an expert witness upon cross-examination or relied upon by the expert witness in direct examination, statements contained in published treatises, periodicals, or pamphlets on a subject of history, medicine, or other science or art, established as a reliable authority by the testimony or admission of the witness or by other expert testimony or by judicial notice. If admitted, the statements may be read into evidence but may not be received as exhibits.

Fed. R. Evid. 706. Court Appointed Experts

(a) Appointment. The court may on its own motion or on the motion of any party enter an order to show cause why expert witnesses should not be appointed, and may request the parties to submit nominations. The court may appoint any expert witnesses agreed upon by the parties, and may appoint expert witnesses of its own selection. An expert witness shall not be appointed by the court unless the witness consents to act. A witness so appointed shall be informed of the witness' duties by the court in writing, a copy of which shall be filed with the clerk, or at a conference in which the parties shall have opportunity to participate. A witness so appointed shall advise the parties of the witness' findings, if any; the witness' deposition may be taken by any party; and the witness may be called to testify by the court or any party. The witness shall be subject to cross-examination by each party, including a party calling the witness.

(b) Compensation. Expert witnesses so appointed are entitled to reasonable compensation in whatever sum the court may allow. The compensation thus fixed is payable from funds which may be provided by law in criminal cases and civil actions and proceedings involving just compensation under the fifth amendment. In other civil actions and proceedings the compensation shall be paid by the parties in such proportion and at such time as the court directs, and thereafter charged in like manner as other costs.

(c) Disclosure of appointment. In the exercise of its discretion, the court may authorize disclosure to the jury of the fact that the court appointed the expert witness.

(d) Parties' experts of own selection. Nothing in this rule limits the parties in

C.E.C. § 730. Appointment of expert by court

When it appears to the court, at any time before or during the trial of an action, that expert evidence is or may be required by the court or by any party to the action, the court on its own motion or on motion of any party may appoint one or more experts to investigate, to render a report as may be ordered by the court, and to testify as an expert at the trial of the action relative to the fact or matter as to which the expert evidence is or may be required. The court may fix the compensation for these services, if any, rendered by any person appointed under this section, in addition to any service as a witness, at the amount as seems reasonable to the court.

Nothing in this section shall be construed to permit a person to perform any act for which a license is required unless the person holds the appropriate license to lawfully perform that act.

C.E.C. § 731. Payment of court-appointed expert

(a) In all criminal actions and juvenile court proceedings, the compensation fixed under Section 730 shall be a charge against the county in which such action or proceeding is pending and shall be paid out of the treasury of such county on order of the court.

(b) In any county in which the board of supervisors so provides, the compensation fixed under Section 730 for medical experts in civil actions in such county shall be a charge against and paid out of the treasury of such county on order of the court.

(c) Except as otherwise provided in this section, in all civil actions, the compensation fixed under Section 730 shall, in the first instance, be apportioned

calling expert witnesses of their own selection.	and charged to the several parties in such proportion as the court may determine and may thereafter be taxed and allowed in like manner as other costs.
	C.E.C. § 732. Calling and examining court-appointed expert Any expert appointed by the court under Section 730 may be called and examined by the court or by any party to the action. When such witness is called and examined by the court, the parties have the same right as is expressed in Section 775 to cross-examine the witness and to object to the questions asked and the evidence adduced.
	C.E.C. § 733. Right to produce other expert evidence Nothing contained in this article shall be deemed or construed to prevent any party to any action from producing other expert evidence on the same fact or matter mentioned in Section 730; but, where other expert witnesses are called by a party to the action, their fees shall be paid by the party calling them and only ordinary witness fees shall be taxed as costs in the action.

CHAPTER
8

Privileges

B.   THE FEDERAL RULE

Fed. R. Evid. 501. General Rule Except as otherwise required by the Constitution of the United States or provided by Act of Congress or in rules prescribed by the Supreme Court pursuant to statutory authority, the privilege of a witness, person, government, State, or political subdivision thereof shall be governed by the principles of the common law as they may be interpreted by the courts of the United States in the light of reason and experience. However, in civil actions and proceedings, with respect to an element of a claim or defense as to which State law supplies the rule of decision, the privilege of a witness, person, government, State, or political subdivision thereof shall be determined in accordance with State law.	**C.E.C. § 911. Refusal to be or have another as witness, or disclose or produce any matter** Except as otherwise provided by statute: (a) No person has a privilege to refuse to be a witness. (b) No person has a privilege to refuse to disclose any matter or to refuse to produce any writing, object, or other thing. (c) No person has a privilege that another shall not be a witness or shall not disclose any matter or shall not produce any writing, object, or other thing.

Question for Classroom Discussion
Casebook page 538

Civil action for personal injuries brought under diversity jurisdiction in a California federal district court. Defendant offers into evidence the testimony of plaintiff's son concerning statements plaintiff made about her personal injuries. Plaintiff objects, arguing that the statements were made in confidence and the court should recognize a privilege for parent-child confidential communications. There is no federal or California statute recognizing such a privilege. How should the court rule on the objection?

C.   GENERAL PRINCIPLES

C.E.C. § 913. Comment on, and inferences from, exercise of privilege

(a) If in the instant proceeding or on a prior occasion a privilege is or was exercised not to testify with respect to any matter, or to refuse to disclose or to prevent another from disclosing any matter, neither the presiding officer nor counsel may comment thereon, no presumption shall arise because of the exercise of the privilege, and the trier of fact may not draw any inference therefrom as to the credibility of the witness or as to any matter at issue in the proceeding.

(b) The court, at the request of a party who may be adversely affected because an unfavorable inference may be drawn by the jury because a privilege has been exercised, shall instruct the jury that no presumption arises because of the exercise of the privilege and that the jury may not draw any inference therefrom as to the credibility of the witness or as to any matter at issue in the proceeding.

C.E.C. § 914. Determination of claim of privilege; limitation on punishment for contempt

(a) The presiding officer shall determine a claim of privilege in any proceeding in the same manner as a court determines such a claim under Article 2 (commencing with Section 400) of Chapter 4 of Division 3.

(b) No person may be held in contempt for failure to disclose information claimed to be privileged unless he has failed to comply with an order of a court that he disclose such information. This subdivision does not apply to any governmental agency that has constitutional contempt power, nor does it apply to hearings and investigations of the Industrial Accident Commission, nor does it impliedly repeal Chapter 4

158

Fed. R. Evid. 104. Preliminary Questions
(a) Questions of admissibility generally. Preliminary questions concerning the qualification of a person to be a witness, the existence of a privilege, or the admissibility of evidence shall be determined by the court, subject to the provisions of subdivision (b). In making its determination it is not bound by the rules of evidence except those with respect to privileges.

(commencing with Section 9400) of Part 1 of Division 2 of Title 2 of the Government Code. If no other statutory procedure is applicable, the procedure prescribed by Section 1991 of the Code of Civil Procedure shall be followed in seeking an order of a court that the person disclose the information claimed to be privileged.

C.E.C. § 915. Disclosure of privileged information or attorney work product in ruling on claim of privilege
(a) Subject to subdivision (b), the presiding officer may not require disclosure of information claimed to be privileged under this division or attorney work product under subdivision (a) of Section 2018.030 of the Code of Civil Procedure in order to rule on the claim of privilege; provided, however, that in any hearing conducted pursuant to subdivision (c) of Section 1524 of the Penal Code in which a claim of privilege is made and the court determines that there is no other feasible means to rule on the validity of the claim other than to require disclosure, the court shall proceed in accordance with subdivision (b).
(b) When a court is ruling on a claim of privilege under Article 9 (commencing with Section 1040) of Chapter 4 (official information and identity of informer) or under Section 1060 (trade secret) or under subdivision (b) of Section 2018.030 of the Code of Civil Procedure (attorney work product) and is unable to do so without requiring disclosure of the information claimed to be privileged, the court may require the person from whom disclosure is sought or the person authorized to claim the privilege, or both, to disclose the information in chambers out of the presence and hearing of all persons except the person authorized to claim the privilege and any other persons as the person authorized to claim the privilege is willing to have present. If the judge determines that

the information is privileged, neither the judge nor any other person may ever disclose, without the consent of a person authorized to permit disclosure, what was disclosed in the course of the proceedings in chambers.

C.E.C. § 916. Exclusion of privileged information where persons authorized to claim privilege are not present
(a) The presiding officer, on his own motion or on the motion of any party, shall exclude information that is subject to a claim of privilege under this division if:
(1) The person from whom the information is sought is not a person authorized to claim the privilege; and
(2) There is no party to the proceeding who is a person authorized to claim the privilege.
(b) The presiding officer may not exclude information under this section if:
(1) He is otherwise instructed by a person authorized to permit disclosure; or
(2) The proponent of the evidence establishes that there is no person authorized to claim the privilege in existence.

C.E.C. § 917. Presumption that certain communications are confidential; privileged character of electronic communications
(a) Whenever a privilege is claimed on the ground that the matter sought to be disclosed is a communication made in confidence in the course of the lawyer-client, physician-patient, psychotherapist-patient, clergy-penitent, husband-wife, sexual assault victim-counselor, or domestic violence victim-counselor relationship, the communication is presumed to have been made in confidence and the opponent of the claim of privilege has the burden of proof to establish that the communication was not confidential.

	(b) A communication between persons in a relationship listed in subdivision (a) does not lose its privileged character for the sole reason that it is communicated by electronic means or because persons involved in the delivery, facilitation, or storage of electronic communication may have access to the content of the communication.
	(c) For purposes of this section, "electronic" has the same meaning provided in Section 1633.2 of the Civil Code.

Question for Classroom Discussion
Casebook page 568

[The following is based on question 4 from page 568 of the casebook.] Civil fraud action. Plaintiff alleges that over the course of several years, Defendant, a financial planner, engaged in a scheme to steal money from her clients. Prior to trial, one of Defendant's former employees approaches Plaintiff and states that Defendant's attorney, Attorney, was "helping Defendant cover up the scam for three weeks just before the scam fell apart." She states that during several of the meetings between Defendant and Attorney, she heard the sound of a shredder working for long periods of time. Plaintiff notifies Attorney that she intends to take Attorney's deposition, and demands that Attorney produce all notes "taken during meetings held with Defendant" during the three-week period. Defendant refuses to produce the notes, asserting attorney-client privilege. Plaintiff responds that the crime-fraud exception applies, and asks the court to take possession of Attorney's notes and conduct an *in camera* inspection to determine whether the crime-fraud exception applies. How should the court proceed under rejected federal law? Under the C.E.C.?

D.   THE ATTORNEY-CLIENT PRIVILEGE

Rejected Rule 503. Lawyer-Client Privilege	
(a) Definitions. As used in this rule: (1) A "client" is a person, public officer, or corporation, association, or other	**C.E.C. § 951. Client** As used in this article, "client" means a person who, directly or through an

organization or entity, either public or private, who is rendered professional legal services by a lawyer, or who consults a lawyer with a view to obtaining professional legal services from him.

(2) A "lawyer" is a person authorized, or reasonably believed by the client to be authorized, to practice law in any state or nation.

(3) A "representative of the lawyer" is one employed to assist the lawyer in the rendition of professional legal services.

(4) A communication is "confidential" if not intended to be disclosed to third persons other than those to whom disclosure is in furtherance of the rendition of professional legal services to the client or those reasonably necessary for the transmission of the communication.

(b) General rule of privilege. A client has a privilege to refuse to disclose and to prevent any other person from disclosing confidential communications made for the purpose of facilitating the rendition of professional legal services to the client, (1) between himself or his representative and

authorized representative, consults a lawyer for the purpose of retaining the lawyer or securing legal service or advice from him in his professional capacity, and includes an incompetent (a) who himself so consults the lawyer or (b) whose guardian or conservator so consults the lawyer in behalf of the incompetent.

C.E.C. § 950. Lawyer
As used in this article, "lawyer" means a person authorized, or reasonably believed by the client to be authorized, to practice law in any state or nation.

C.E.C. § 952. Confidential communication between client and lawyer
As used in this article, "confidential communication between client and lawyer" means information transmitted between a client and his or her lawyer in the course of that relationship and in confidence by a means which, so far as the client is aware, discloses the information to no third persons other than those who are present to further the interest of the client in the consultation or those to whom disclosure is reasonably necessary for the transmission of the information or the accomplishment of the purpose for which the lawyer is consulted, and includes a legal opinion formed and the advice given by the lawyer in the course of that relationship.

C.E.C. § 954. Lawyer-client privilege
Subject to Section 912 and except as otherwise provided in this article, the client, whether or not a party, has a privilege to refuse to disclose, and to prevent another from disclosing, a confidential communication between client

his lawyer or his lawyer's representative, or (2) between his lawyer and the lawyer's representative, or (3) by him or his lawyer to a lawyer representing another in a matter of common interest, or (4) between representatives of the client or between the client and a representative of the client, or (5) between lawyers representing the client.

(c) Who may claim the privilege. The privilege may be claimed by the client, his guardian or conservator, the personal representative of a deceased client, or the successor, trustee, or similar representative of a corporation, association, or other organization, whether or not in existence. The person who was the lawyer at the time of the communication may claim the privilege but only on behalf of the client. His authority to do so is presumed in the absence of evidence to the contrary.

and lawyer if the privilege is claimed by:
(a) The holder of the privilege;
(b) A person who is authorized to claim the privilege by the holder of the privilege; or
(c) The person who was the lawyer at the time of the confidential communication, but such person may not claim the privilege if there is no holder of the privilege in existence or if he is otherwise instructed by a person authorized to permit disclosure. The relationship of attorney and client shall exist between a law corporation as defined in Article 10 (commencing with Section 6160) of Chapter 4 of Division 3 of the Business and Professions Code and the persons to whom it renders professional services, as well as between such persons and members of the State Bar employed by such corporation to render services to such persons. The word "persons" as used in this subdivision includes partnerships, corporations, limited liability companies, associations and other groups and entities.

C.E.C. § 953. Holder of the privilege
As used in this article, "holder of the privilege" means:
(a) The client when he has no guardian or conservator.
(b) A guardian or conservator of the client when the client has a guardian or conservator.
(c) The personal representative of the client if the client is dead.
(d) A successor, assign, trustee in dissolution, or any similar representative of a firm, association, organization, partnership, business trust, corporation, or public entity that is no longer in existence.

C.E.C. § 955. When lawyer required to claim privilege
The lawyer who received or made a communication subject to the privilege under this article shall claim the privilege whenever he is present when the

(d) Exceptions. There is no privilege under this rule: (1) Furtherance of crime or fraud. If the services of the lawyer were sought or obtained to enable or aid anyone to commit or plan to commit what the client knew or reasonably should have known to be a crime or fraud; or	communication is sought to be disclosed and is authorized to claim the privilege under subdivision (c) of Section 954. **C.E.C. § 956. Exception: Crime or fraud** There is no privilege under this article if the services of the lawyer were sought or obtained to enable or aid anyone to commit or plan to commit a crime or a fraud.
(2) Claimants through same deceased client. As to a communication relevant to an issue between parties who claim through the same deceased client, regardless of whether the claims are by testate or intestate succession or by *inter vivos* transaction; or	**C.E.C. § 957. Exception: Parties claiming through deceased client** There is no privilege under this article as to a communication relevant to an issue between parties all of whom claim through a deceased client, regardless of whether the claims are by testate or intestate succession or by inter vivos transaction.
	C.E.C. § 960. Exception: Intention of deceased client concerning writing affecting property interest There is no privilege under this article as to a communication relevant to an issue concerning the intention of a client, now deceased, with respect to a deed of conveyance, will, or other writing, executed by the client, purporting to affect an interest in property.
	C.E.C. § 961. Exception: Validity of writing affecting property interest There is no privilege under this article as to a communication relevant to an issue concerning the validity of a deed of conveyance, will, or other writing, executed by a client, now deceased, purporting to affect an interest in property.
(3) Breach of duty by lawyer or client. As to a communication relevant to an issue of breach of duty by the lawyer to his client or by the client to his lawyer; or	**C.E.C. § 958. Exception: Breach of duty arising out of lawyer-client relationship** There is no privilege under this article as to a communication relevant to an issue of

	breach, by the lawyer or by the client, of a duty arising out of the lawyer-client relationship.
(4) Document attested by lawyer. As to a communication relevant to an issue concerning an attested document to which the lawyer is an attesting witness; or	**C.E.C. § 959. Exception: Lawyer as attesting witness** There is no privilege under this article as to a communication relevant to an issue concerning the intention or competence of a client executing an attested document of which the lawyer is an attesting witness, or concerning the execution or attestation of such a document.
(5) Joint clients. As to a communication relevant to a matter of common interest between two or more clients if the communication was made by any of them to a lawyer retained or consulted in common, when offered in an action between any of the clients.	**C.E.C. § 962. Exception: Joint clients** Where two or more clients have retained or consulted a lawyer upon a matter of common interest, none of them, nor the successor in interest of any of them, may claim a privilege under this article as to a communication made in the course of that relationship when such communication is offered in a civil proceeding between one of such clients (or his successor in interest) and another of such clients (or his successor in interest).
	C.E.C. § 956.5. Reasonable belief that disclosure of confidential communication relating to representation of client is necessary to prevent criminal act that lawyer reasonably believes likely to result in death of, or substantial bodily harm to, an individual; exception to privilege There is no privilege under this article if the lawyer reasonably believes that disclosure of any confidential communication relating to representation of a client is necessary to prevent a criminal act that the lawyer reasonably believes is likely to result in the death of, or substantial bodily harm to, an individual.

E.   MEDICAL PRIVILEGES

Rejected Rule 504. Patient's Privilege **(a) Definitions.** (1) A "patient" is a person who consults or is examined or interviewed by a psychotherapist.	**C.E.C. § 1011. Patient** As used in this article, "patient" means a person who consults a psychotherapist or submits to an examination by a psychotherapist for the purpose of securing a diagnosis or preventive, palliative, or curative treatment of his mental or emotional condition or who submits to an examination of his mental or emotional condition for the purpose of scientific research on mental or emotional problems.
(2) A "psychotherapist" is (A) a person authorized to practice medicine in any state or nation, or reasonably believed by the patient so to be, while engaged in the diagnosis or treatment of a mental or emotional condition, including drug addiction, or (B) a person licensed or certified as a psychologist under the laws of any state or nation, while similarly engaged.	**C.E.C. § 1010. Psychotherapist** As used in this article, "psychotherapist" means a person who is, or is reasonably believed by the patient to be: (a) A person authorized to practice medicine in any state or nation who devotes, or is reasonably believed by the patient to devote, a substantial portion of his or her time to the practice of psychiatry. (b) A person licensed as a psychologist under Chapter 6.6 (commencing with Section 2900) of Division 2 of the Business and Professions Code.

(c) A person licensed as a clinical social worker under Article 4 (commencing with Section 4996) of Chapter 14 of Division 2 of the Business and Professions Code, when he or she is engaged in applied psychotherapy of a nonmedical nature.

(d) A person who is serving as a school psychologist and holds a credential authorizing that service issued by the state.

(e) A person licensed as a marriage and family therapist under Chapter 13 (commencing with Section 4980) of Division 2 of the Business and Professions Code.

(f) A person registered as a psychological assistant who is under the supervision of a licensed psychologist or board certified psychiatrist as required by Section 2913 of the Business and Professions Code, or a person registered as a marriage and family therapist intern who is under the supervision of a licensed marriage and family therapist, a licensed clinical social worker, a licensed psychologist, or a licensed physician certified in psychiatry, as specified in Section 4980.44 of the Business and Professions Code.

(g) A person registered as an associate clinical social worker who is under the supervision of a licensed clinical social worker, a licensed psychologist, or a board certified psychiatrist as required by Section 4996.20 or 4996.21 of the Business and Professions Code.

(h) A person exempt from the Psychology Licensing Law pursuant to subdivision (d) of Section 2909 of the Business and Professions Code who is under the supervision of a licensed psychologist or board certified psychiatrist.

(i) A psychological intern as defined in Section 2911 of the Business and Professions Code who is under the supervision of a licensed psychologist or board certified psychiatrist.

(j) A trainee, as defined in subdivision (c)

of Section 4980.03 of the Business and Professions Code, who is fulfilling his or her supervised practicum required by subdivision (b) of Section 4980.40 of the Business and Professions Code and is supervised by a licensed psychologist, board certified psychiatrist, a licensed clinical social worker, or a licensed marriage and family therapist.

(k) A person licensed as a registered nurse pursuant to Chapter 6 (commencing with Section 2700) of Division 2 of the Business and Professions Code, who possesses a master's degree in psychiatric-mental health nursing and is listed as a psychiatric-mental health nurse by the Board of Registered Nursing.

(l) An advanced practice registered nurse who is certified as a clinical nurse specialist pursuant to Article 9 (commencing with Section 2838) of Chapter 6 of Division 2 of the Business and Professions Code and who participates in expert clinical practice in the specialty of psychiatric-mental health nursing.

(m) A person rendering mental health treatment or counseling services as authorized pursuant to Section 6924 of the Family Code.

C.E.C. § 1012. Confidential communication between patient and psychotherapist

(3) A communication is "confidential" if not intended to be disclosed to third persons other than those present to further the interest of the patient in the consultation, examination, or interview, or persons reasonably necessary for the transmission of the communication, or persons who are participating in the diagnosis and treatment under the direction of the psychotherapist, including members of the patient's family.

As used in this article, "confidential communication between patient and psychotherapist" means information, including information obtained by an examination of the patient, transmitted between a patient and his psychotherapist in the course of that relationship and in confidence by a means which, so far as the patient is aware, discloses the information to no third persons other than those who are present to further the interest of the patient in the consultation, or those to whom disclosure is reasonably necessary

(b) General Rule of Privilege. A patient has a privilege to refuse to disclose and to prevent any other person from disclosing confidential communications, made for the purposes of diagnosis or treatment of his mental or emotional condition, including drug addiction, among himself, his psychotherapist, or persons who are participating in the diagnosis or treatment under the direction of the psychotherapist, including members of the patient's family.

for the transmission of the information or the accomplishment of the purpose for which the psychotherapist is consulted, and includes a diagnosis made and the advice given by the psychotherapist in the course of that relationship.

C.E.C. § 1014. Psychotherapist-patient privilege; application to individuals and entities

Subject to Section 912 and except as otherwise provided in this article, the patient, whether or not a party, has a privilege to refuse to disclose, and to prevent another from disclosing, a confidential communication between patient and psychotherapist if the privilege is claimed by:

(a) The holder of the privilege.

(b) A person who is authorized to claim the privilege by the holder of the privilege.

(c) The person who was the psychotherapist at the time of the confidential communication, but the person may not claim the privilege if there is no holder

of the privilege in existence or if he or she is otherwise instructed by a person authorized to permit disclosure.

The relationship of a psychotherapist and patient shall exist between a psychological corporation as defined in Article 9 (commencing with Section 2995) of Chapter 6.6 of Division 2 of the Business and Professions Code, a marriage and family therapy corporation as defined in Article 6 (commencing with Section 4987.5) of Chapter 13 of Division 2 of the Business and Professions Code, or a licensed clinical social workers corporation as defined in Article 5 (commencing with Section 4998) of Chapter 14 of Division 2 of the Business and Professions Code, and the patient to whom it renders professional services, as well as between those patients and psychotherapists employed by those

(c) Who May Claim the Privilege.
The privilege may be claimed by the patient, by his guardian or conservator, or by the personal representative of a deceased patient. The person who was the psychotherapist may claim the privilege but only on behalf of the patient. His authority so to do is presumed in the absence of evidence to the contrary.

(d) Exceptions.
(1) Proceedings for Hospitalization. There is no privilege under this rule for communications relevant to an issue in proceedings to hospitalize the patient for mental illness, if the psychotherapist in the course of diagnosis or treatment has determined that the patient is in need of hospitalization.

(2) Examination by Order of Judge. If the judge orders an examination of the mental or emotional condition of the patient, communications made in the course thereof are not privileged under this rule with respect to the particular purpose for which the examination is ordered unless the judge orders otherwise.

corporations to render services to those patients. The word "persons" as used in this subdivision includes partnerships, corporations, limited liability companies, associations and other groups and entities.

C.E.C. § 1013. Holder of the privilege
As used in this article, "holder of the privilege" means:
(a) The patient when he has no guardian or conservator.
(b) A guardian or conservator of the patient when the patient has a guardian or conservator.
(c) The personal representative of the patient if the patient is dead.

C.E.C. § 1015. When psychotherapist required to claim privilege
The psychotherapist who received or made a communication subject to the privilege under this article shall claim the privilege whenever he is present when the communication is sought to be disclosed and is authorized to claim the privilege under subdivision (c) of Section 1014.

C.E.C. § 1024. Exception: Patient dangerous to himself or others
There is no privilege under this article if the psychotherapist has reasonable cause to believe that the patient is in such mental or emotional condition as to be dangerous to himself or to the person or property of another and that disclosure of the communication is necessary to prevent the threatened danger.

C.E.C. § 1017. Exception: Psychotherapist appointed by court or board of prison terms
(a) There is no privilege under this article if the psychotherapist is appointed by order of a court to examine the patient, but this exception does not apply where the psychotherapist is appointed by order of

the court upon the request of the lawyer for the defendant in a criminal proceeding in order to provide the lawyer with information needed so that he or she may advise the defendant whether to enter or withdraw a plea based on insanity or to present a defense based on his or her mental or emotional condition.

(b) There is no privilege under this article if the psychotherapist is appointed by the Board of Prison Terms to examine a patient pursuant to the provisions of Article 4 (commencing with Section 2960) of Chapter 7 of Title 1 of Part 3 of the Penal Code.

(3) Condition an Element of Claim or Defense. There is no privilege under this rule as to communications relevant to an issue of the mental or emotional condition of the patient in any proceeding in which he relies upon the condition as an element of his claim or defense, or, after the patient's death, in any proceeding in which any party relies upon the condition as an element of his claim or defense.

C.E.C. § 1016. Exception: Patient-litigant exception
There is no privilege under this article as to a communication relevant to an issue concerning the mental or emotional condition of the patient if such issue has been tendered by:
(a) The patient;
(b) Any party claiming through or under the patient;
(c) Any party claiming as a beneficiary of the patient through a contract to which the patient is or was a party; or
(d) The plaintiff in an action brought under Section 376 or 377 of the Code of Civil Procedure for damages for the injury or death of the patient.

C.E.C. § 1018. Exception: Crime or tort
There is no privilege under this article if the services of the psychotherapist were sought or obtained to enable or aid anyone to commit or plan to commit a crime or a tort or to escape detection or apprehension after the commission of a crime or a tort.

C.E.C. § 1019. Exception: Parties claiming through deceased patient
There s no privilege under this article as to a communication relevant to an issue

between parties all of whom claim through a deceased patient, regardless of whether the claims are by testate or intestate succession or by inter vivos transaction.

C.E.C. § 1020. Exception: Breach of duty arising out of psychotherapist-patient relationship
There is no privilege under this article as to a communication relevant to an issue of breach, by the psychotherapist or by the patient, of a duty arising out of the psychotherapist-patient relationship.

C.E.C. § 1021. Exception: Intention of deceased patient concerning writing affecting property interest
There is no privilege under this article as to a communication relevant to an issue concerning the intention of a patient, now deceased, with respect to a deed of conveyance, will, or other writing, executed by the patient, purporting to affect an interest in property.

C.E.C. § 1022. Exception: Validity of writing affecting property interest
There is no privilege under this article as to a communication relevant to an issue concerning the validity of a deed of conveyance, will, or other writing, executed by a patient, now deceased, purporting to affect an interest in property.

C.E.C. § 1023. Exception: Proceeding to determine sanity of criminal defendant
There is no privilege under this article in a proceeding under Chapter 6 (commencing with Section 1367) of Title 10 of Part 2 of the Penal Code initiated at the request of the defendant in a criminal action to determine his sanity.

C.E.C. § 1025. Exception: Proceeding to establish competence

There is no privilege under this article in a proceeding brought by or on behalf of the patient to establish his competence.

C.E.C. § 1026. Exception: Required report

There is no privilege under this article as to information that the psychotherapist or the patient is required to report to a public employee or as to information required to be recorded in a public office, if such report or record is open to public inspection.

C.E.C. § 1027. Exception: Child under 16 victim of crime

There is no privilege under this article if all of the following circumstances exist:
(a) The patient is a child under the age of 16.
(b) The psychotherapist has reasonable cause to believe that the patient has been the victim of a crime and that disclosure of the communication is in the best interest of the child.

C.E.C. § 990. Physician

As used in this article, "physician" means a person authorized, or reasonably believed by the patient to be authorized, to practice medicine in any state or nation.

C.E.C. § 991. Patient

As used in this article, "patient" means a person who consults a physician or submits to an examination by a physician for the purpose of securing a diagnosis or preventive, palliative, or curative treatment of his physical or mental or emotional condition.

C.E.C. § 992. Confidential communication between patient and physician

As used in this article, "confidential communication between patient and physician" means information, including information obtained by an examination of the patient, transmitted between a patient and his physician in the course of that relationship and in confidence by a means which, so far as the patient is aware, discloses the information to no third persons other than those who are present to further the interest of the patient in the consultation or those to whom disclosure is reasonably necessary for the transmission of the information or the accomplishment of the purpose for which the physician is consulted, and includes a diagnosis made and the advice given by the physician in the course of that relationship.

C.E.C. § 993. Holder of the privilege

As used in this article, "holder of the privilege" means:

(a) The patient when he has no guardian or conservator.

(b) A guardian or conservator of the patient when the patient has a guardian or conservator

(c) The personal representative of the patient if the patient is dead.

C.E.C. § 994. Physician-patient privilege

Subject to Section 912 and except as otherwise provided in this article, the patient, whether or not a party, has a privilege to refuse to disclose, and to prevent another from disclosing, a confidential communication between patient and physician if the privilege is claimed by

(a) The holder of the privilege;

(b) A person who is authorized to claim the privilege by the holder of the privilege; or

(c) The person who was the physician at

the time of the confidential communication, but such person may not claim the privilege if there is no holder of the privilege in existence or if he or she is otherwise instructed by a person authorized to permit disclosure. The relationship of a physician and patient shall exist between a medical or podiatry corporation as defined in the Medical Practice Act and the patient to whom it renders professional services, as well as between such patients and licensed physicians and surgeons employed by such corporation to render services to such patients. The word "persons" as used in this subdivision includes partnerships, corporations, limited liability companies, associations, and other groups and entities.

C.E.C. § 995. When physician required to claim privilege
The physician who received or made a communication subject to the privilege under this article shall claim the privilege whenever he is present when the communication is sought to be disclosed and is authorized to claim the privilege under subdivision (c) of Section 994

C.E.C. § 996. Patient-litigant exception
There is no privilege under this article as to a communication relevant to an issue concerning the condition of the patient if such issue has been tendered by:
(a) The patient;
(b) Any party claiming through or under the patient;
(c) Any party claiming as a beneficiary of the patient through a contract to which the patient is or was a party; or
(d) The plaintiff in an action brought under Section 376 or 377 of the Code of Civil Procedure for damages for the injury or death of the patient.

C.E.C. § 997. Exception: crime or tort
There is no privilege under this article if

the services of the physician were sought or obtained to enable or aid anyone to commit or plan to commit a crime or a tort or to escape detection or apprehension after the commission of a crime or a tort.

C.E.C. § 998. Criminal proceeding
There is no privilege under this article in a criminal proceeding.

C.E.C. § 999. Communication relating to patient condition in proceeding to recover damages; good cause
There is no privilege under this article as to a communication relevant to an issue concerning the condition of the patient in a proceeding to recover damages on account of the conduct of the patient if good cause for disclosure of the communication is shown.

C.E.C. § 1000. Parties claiming through deceased patient
There is no privilege under this article as to a communication relevant to an issue between parties all of whom claim through a deceased patient, regardless of whether the claims are by testate or intestate succession or by inter vivos transaction.

C.E.C. § 1001. Breach of duty arising out of physician-patient relationship
There is no privilege under this article as to a communication relevant to an issue of breach, by the physician or by the patient, of a duty arising out of the physician-patient relationship.

C.E.C. § 1002. Intention of deceased patient concerning writing affecting property interest
There is no privilege under this article as to a communication relevant to an issue concerning the intention of a patient, now deceased, with respect to a deed of conveyance, will, or other writing,

executed by the patient, purporting to affect an interest in property.

C.E.C. § 1003. Validity of writing affecting property interest
There is no privilege under this article as to a communication relevant to an issue concerning the validity of a deed of conveyance, will, or other writing, executed by a patient, now deceased, purporting to affect an interest in property.

C.E.C. § 1004. Commitment or similar proceeding
There is no privilege under this article in a proceeding to commit the patient or otherwise place him or his property, or both, under the control of another because of his alleged mental or physical condition.

C.E.C. § 1005. Proceeding to establish competence
There is no privilege under this article in a proceeding brought by or on behalf of the patient to establish his competence.

C.E.C. § 1006. Required report
There is no privilege under this article as to information that the physician or the patient is required to report to a public employee, or as to information required to be recorded in a public office, if such report or record is open to public inspection.

C.E.C. § 1007. Proceeding to terminate right, license or privilege
There is no privilege under this article in a proceeding brought by a public entity to determine whether a right, authority, license, or privilege (including the right or privilege to be employed by the public entity or to hold a public office) should be revoked, suspended, terminated, limited, or conditioned.

	C.E.C. § 1035.8. Sexual assault victim-counselor privilege A victim of a sexual assault, whether or not a party, has a privilege to refuse to disclose, and to prevent another from disclosing, a confidential communication between the victim and a sexual assault victim counselor if the privilege is claimed by: (a) The holder of the privilege; (b) A person who is authorized to claim the privilege by the holder of the privilege; or (c) The person who was the sexual assault victim counselor at the time of the confidential communication, but such person may not claim the privilege if there is no holder of the privilege in existence or if he is otherwise instructed by a person authorized to permit disclosure. **C.E.C. § 1037.5. Privilege of refusal to disclose communication; claimants** A victim of domestic violence, whether or not a party to the action, has a privilege to refuse to disclose, and to prevent another from disclosing, a confidential communication between the victim and a domestic violence counselor if the privilege is claimed by any of the following persons: (a) The holder of the privilege. (b) A person who is authorized to claim the privilege by the holder of the privilege. (c) The person who was the domestic violence counselor at the time of the confidential communication. However, that person may not claim the privilege if there is no holder of the privilege in existence or if he or she is otherwise instructed by a person authorized to permit disclosure.

[Following are the questions appearing on pages 582-583 of the casebook adapted for use with the pertinent sections of the C.E.C.]

1. Plaintiff sues Defendant for negligence following a collision between their two vehicles. After the accident, Plaintiff sought treatment for her injuries from Doctor, an orthopedic physician. Prior to trial, Defendant takes the deposition of Doctor, and asks Doctor to produce all records relating to the treatment of Plaintiff for injuries allegedly sustained in the accident. Doctor refuses to produce the papers, and refuses to answer any questions relating to injuries sustained in the accident. Defendant asks the court to order Doctor to produce the papers and to answer Defendant's questions. How should the court rule under the C.E.C.?

2. Same case. Assume Doctor was Plaintiff's orthopedic specialist before the accident as well as after. At the deposition, Defendant asks Doctor to disclose any treatment of Plaintiff prior to the collision. Does the privilege apply under the C.E.C.?

3. Same case. Plaintiff's attorney asks Plaintiff to visit Ortho, a different orthopedic specialist, to help the attorney prepare for trial. Plaintiff does so, and Ortho sends the attorney a report concerning Plaintiff's condition. Plaintiff's attorney does not plan to call Ortho as a witness at trial. Defendant seeks to take Ortho's deposition, and demands that Ortho produce a copy of the report she sent Plaintiff's attorney. Must Ortho comply under the C.E.C.?

4. Vehicular homicide prosecution. At trial, the prosecutor calls Witness, who was crossing the street with Victim. Witness was the only eyewitness to the accident other than Defendant. Witness testifies that Defendant drove through a red light and struck and killed Victim, who was crossing the street, and that Defendant's car narrowly missed Witness. Defendant testifies that she was driving properly and that Victim and Witness had darted out in front of her car. Defendant wishes to establish that Witness suffers from a mental condition that causes her not to be able to distinguish reality from fantasy, and that this condition led Witness to give an incorrect version of the facts. To establish this, Defendant calls Witness's psychiatrist and asks her about her treatment of Witness. The prosecutor objects on grounds of the psychotherapist-patient privilege. How should the court rule?

5. Proceeding to determine the competence of Defendant to stand trial for a crime. Prior to the hearing, the court appointed Psych, a psychiatrist, to conduct a mental evaluation of Defendant. At the hearing, Defendant raises a privilege objection to

Psych's testimony about the sessions Defendant and Psych had together. How should the court rule under the C.E.C.?

6. Proceeding to probate the will of Deceased. One party challenges the will on the ground Deceased was not competent to make a will at the time she signed it. To prove lack of competence, the party calls Psych, who had been Deceased's psychiatrist in the months prior to her death, to testify about Deceased's mental condition. The other party objects on grounds of the psychotherapist-patient privilege. How should the court rule under the C.E.C.?

7. Prosecution of Defendant for attempted murder of Victim. At trial, the prosecution calls Psych, a psychiatrist who had been treating Defendant in the months prior to the alleged attempted murder. The prosecutor asks Psych if, during one of their sessions, Defendant said, "I should kill Victim if I ever have a chance." Defendant objects on grounds of privilege. How should the court rule under the C.E.C.?

F.   CLERGY PRIVILEGE

Rejected Rule 506	C.E.C. § 1030. Member of the clergy
(a) Definitions. As used in this rule: (1) A "clergyman" is a minister, priest, rabbi, or other similar functionary of a religious organization, or an individual reasonably believed so to be by the person consulting him. (2) A communication is "confidential" if made privately and not intended for further disclosure except to other persons present in furtherance of the purpose of the communication.	As used in this article, a "member of the clergy" means a priest, minister, religious practitioner, or similar functionary of a church or of a religious denomination or religious organization. **C.E.C. § 1031. Penitent** As used in this article, "penitent" means a person who has made a penitential communication to a member of the clergy. **C.E.C. § 1032. Penitential communication** As used in this article, "penitential communication" means a communication made in confidence, in the presence of no third person so far as the penitent is aware, to a member of the clergy who, in the course of the discipline or practice of the clergy member's church, denomination, or organization, is authorized or accustomed to hear those communications and, under the discipline or tenets of his or her church,

180

(b) General rule of privilege. A person has a privilege to refuse to disclose and to prevent another from disclosing a confidential communication by the person to a clergyman in his professional character as spiritual adviser. **(c) Who may claim the privilege.** The privilege may be claimed by the person, by his guardian or conservator, or by his personal representative if he is deceased. The clergyman may claim the privilege on behalf of the person. His authority so to do is presumed in the absence of evidence to the contrary.	denomination, or organization, has a duty to keep those communications secret. **C.E.C. § 1033. Privilege of penitent** Subject to Section 912, a penitent, whether or not a party, has a privilege to refuse to disclose, and to prevent another from disclosing, a penitential communication if he or she claims the privilege. **C.E.C. § 1034. Privilege of clergy** Subject to Section 912, a member of the clergy, whether or not a party, has a privilege to refuse to disclose a penitential communication if he or she claims the privilege.

G.   SPOUSAL PRIVILEGES

2.   *The Privilege for Confidential Communications Between Spouses*

	C.E.C. § 980. Confidential marital communication privilege Subject to Section 912 and except as otherwise provided in this article, a spouse (or his guardian or conservator when he has a guardian or conservator), whether or not a party, has a privilege during the marital relationship and afterwards to refuse to disclose, and to prevent another from disclosing, a communication if he claims the privilege and the communication was made in confidence between him and the other spouse while they were husband and wife. **C.E.C. § 981. Exception: Crime or fraud** There is no privilege under this article if the communication was made, in whole or in part, to enable or aid anyone to commit or plan to commit a crime or a fraud.

C.E.C. § 982. Commitment or similar proceedings
There is no privilege under this article in a proceeding to commit either spouse or otherwise place him or his property, or both, under the control of another because of his alleged mental or physical condition.

C.E.C. § 983. Competency proceedings
There is no privilege under this article in a proceeding brought by or on behalf of either spouse to establish his competence.

C.E.C. § 984. Proceeding between spouses
There is no privilege under this article in:
(a) A proceeding brought by or on behalf of one spouse against the other spouse.
(b) A proceeding between a surviving spouse and a person who claims through the deceased spouse, regardless of whether such claim is by testate or intestate succession or by inter vivos transaction.

C.E.C. § 985. Criminal proceedings
There is no privilege under this article in a criminal proceeding in which one spouse is charged with:
(a) A crime committed at any time against the person or property of the other spouse or of a child of either.
(b) A crime committed at any time against the person or property of a third person committed in the course of committing a crime against the person or property of the other spouse.
(c) Bigamy.
(d) A crime defined by Section 270 or 270a of the Penal Code.

C.E.C. § 986. Juvenile court proceedings
There is no privilege under this article in a proceeding under the Juvenile Court Law, Chapter 2 (commencing with Section 200) of Part 1 of Division 2 of the Welfare and Institutions Code.

	C.E.C. § 987. Communication offered by spouse who is criminal defendant There is no privilege under this article in a criminal proceeding in which the communication is offered in evidence by a defendant who is one of the spouses between whom the communication was made.

3. *The Adverse Testimony Privilege*

Rejected Rule 505 **(a) General rule of privilege.** An accused in a criminal proceeding has a privilege to prevent his spouse from testifying against him.	**C.E.C. § 970. Spouse's privilege not to testify against spouse; exceptions** Except as otherwise provided by statute, a married person has a privilege not to testify against his spouse in any proceeding.
(b) Who may claim the privilege. The privilege may be claimed by the accused or by the spouse on his behalf. The authority of the spouse to do so is presumed in the absence of evidence to the contrary.	**C.E.C. § 971. Privilege not to be called as a witness against spouse** Except as otherwise provided by statute, a married person whose spouse is a party to a proceeding has a privilege not to be called as a witness by an adverse party to that proceeding without the prior express consent of the spouse having the privilege under this section unless the party calling the spouse does so in good faith without knowledge of the marital relationship.
(c) Exceptions. There is no privilege under this rule (1) in proceedings in which one spouse is charged with a crime against the person or property of the other or of a child of either, or with a crime against the person or property of a third person committed in the course of committing a crime against the other, or (2) as to matters occurring prior to the marriage, or (3) in proceedings in which a spouse is charged with importing an alien for prostitution or other immoral purpose in violation of 8 U.S.C. § 1328, with transporting a female in	**C.E.C. § 972. Exceptions to privilege** A married person does not have a privilege under this article in: (a) A proceeding brought by or on behalf of one spouse against the other spouse. (b) A proceeding to commit or otherwise place his or her spouse or his or her spouse's property, or both, under the control of another because of the spouse's alleged mental or physical condition. (c) A proceeding brought by or on behalf of a spouse to establish his or her competence. (d) A proceeding under the Juvenile Court Law, Chapter 2 (commencing with Section

interstate commerce for immoral purposes or other offense in violation of 18 U.S.C. §§ 2421-2424, or with violation of other similar statutes.

200) of Part 1 of Division 2 of the Welfare and Institutions Code.

(e) A criminal proceeding in which one spouse is charged with:

(1) A crime against the person or property of the other spouse or of a child, parent, relative, or cohabitant of either, whether committed before or during marriage.

(2) A crime against the person or property of a third person committed in the course of committing a crime against the person or property of the other spouse, whether committed before or during marriage.

(3) Bigamy.

(4) A crime defined by Section 270 or 270a of the Penal Code.

(f) A proceeding resulting from a criminal act which occurred prior to legal marriage of the spouses to each other regarding knowledge acquired prior to that marriage if prior to the legal marriage the witness spouse was aware that his or her spouse had been arrested for or had been formally charged with the crime or crimes about which the spouse is called to testify.

(g) A proceeding brought against the spouse by a former spouse so long as the property and debts of the marriage have not been adjudicated, or in order to establish, modify, or enforce a child, family or spousal support obligation arising from the marriage to the former spouse; in a proceeding brought against a spouse by the other parent in order to establish, modify, or enforce a child support obligation for a child of a nonmarital relationship of the spouse; or in a proceeding brought against a spouse by the guardian of a child of that spouse in order to establish, modify, or enforce a child support obligation of the spouse. The married person does not have a privilege under this subdivision to refuse to provide information relating to the issues of income, expenses, assets, debts, and employment of either spouse, but may assert the privilege as otherwise provided

	in this article if other information is requested by the former spouse, guardian, or other parent of the child.
	Any person demanding the otherwise privileged information made available by this subdivision, who also has an obligation to support the child for whom an order to establish, modify, or enforce child support is sought, waives his or her marital privilege to the same extent as the spouse as provided in this subdivision.
	C.E.C. § 973. Waiver of privilege
	(a) Unless erroneously compelled to do so, a married person who testifies in a proceeding to which his spouse is a party, or who testifies against his spouse in any proceeding, does not have a privilege under this article in the proceeding in which such testimony is given.
	(b) There is no privilege under this article in a civil proceeding brought or defended by a married person for the immediate benefit of his spouse or of himself and his spouse.

CHAPTER
9

Burdens of Proof and Presumptions

A.   BURDENS OF PROOF

C.E.C. § 500. Party who has the burden of proof
Except as otherwise provided by law, a party has the burden of proof as to each fact the existence or nonexistence of which is essential to the claim for relief or defense that he is asserting.

C.E.C. § 501. Criminal actions; statutory assignment of burden of proof; controlling section
Insofar as any statute, except Section 522, assigns the burden of proof in a criminal action, such statute is subject to Penal Code Section 1096.

C.E.C. § 502. Instructions on burden of proof
The court on all proper occasions shall instruct the jury as to which party bears the burden of proof on each issue and as to whether that burden requires that a party raise a reasonable doubt concerning the existence or nonexistence of a fact or that he establish the existence or nonexistence of a fact by a preponderance of the evidence, by clear and convincing proof, or by proof beyond a reasonable doubt.

C.E.C. § 520. Claim that person guilty of crime or wrongdoing
The party claiming that a person is guilty of crime or wrongdoing has the burden of proof on that issue.

C.E.C. § 521. Claim that person did not exercise care

The party claiming that a person did not exercise a requisite degree of care has the burden of proof on that issue.

C.E.C. § 522. Claim that person is or was insane

The party claiming that any person, including himself, is or was insane has the burden of proof on that issue.

C.E.C. § 523. Historic locations of water; claims involving state land patents or grants

In any action where the state is a party, regardless of who is the moving party, where (a) the boundary of land patented or otherwise granted by the state is in dispute, or (b) the validity of any state patent or grant dated prior to 1950 is in dispute, the state shall have the burden of proof on all issues relating to the historic locations of rivers, streams, and other water bodies and the authority of the state in issuing the patent or grant.

This section is not intended to nor shall it be construed to supersede existing statutes governing disputes where the state is a party and regarding title to real property.

C.E.C. § 550. Party who has the burden of producing evidence

(a) The burden of producing evidence as to a particular fact is on the party against whom a finding on that fact would be required in the absence of further evidence.
(b) The burden of producing evidence as to a particular fact is initially on the party with the burden of proof as to that fact.

B.   PRESUMPTIONS

Fed. R. Evid. 301. Presumptions In General In Civil Actions And Proceedings
In all civil actions and proceedings not otherwise provided for by Act of Congress or by these rules, a presumption imposes on the party against whom it is directed the burden of going forward with evidence to rebut or meet the presumption, but does not shift to such party the burden of proof in the sense of the risk of nonpersuasion, which remains throughout the trial upon the party on whom it was originally cast.

C.E.C. § 600. Presumption and inference defined
(a) A presumption is an assumption of fact that the law requires to be made from another fact or group of facts found or otherwise established in the action. A presumption is not evidence.
(b) An inference is a deduction of fact that may logically and reasonably be drawn from another fact or group of facts found or otherwise established in the action.

C.E.C. § 601. Classification of presumptions
A presumption is either conclusive or rebuttable. Every rebuttable presumption is either (a) a presumption affecting the burden of producing evidence or (b) a presumption affecting the burden of proof.

C.E.C. § 602. Statute making one fact prima facie evidence of another fact
A statute providing that a fact or group of facts is prima facie evidence of another fact establishes a rebuttable presumption.

C.E.C. § 603. Presumption affecting the burden of producing evidence defined
A presumption affecting the burden of producing evidence is a presumption established to implement no public policy other than to facilitate the determination of the particular action in which the presumption is applied.

C.E.C. § 604. Effect of presumption affecting burden of producing evidence
The effect of a presumption affecting the burden of producing evidence is to require the trier of fact to assume the existence of the presumed fact unless and until evidence is introduced which would support a finding of its nonexistence, in which case

189

Fed. R. Evid. 302. Applicability Of State Law In Civil Actions And Proceedings
In civil actions and proceedings, the effect of a presumption respecting a fact which is an element of a claim or defense as to which state law supplies the rule of decision is determined in accordance with state law.

the trier of fact shall determine the existence or nonexistence of the presumed fact from the evidence and without regard to the presumption. Nothing in this section shall be construed to prevent the drawing of any inference that may be appropriate.

C.E.C. § 605. Presumption affecting the burden of proof defined
A presumption affecting the burden of proof is a presumption established to implement some public policy other than to facilitate the determination of the particular action in which the presumption is applied, such as the policy in favor of establishment of a parent and child relationship, the validity of marriage, the stability of titles to property, or the security of those who entrust themselves or their property to the administration of others.

C.E.C. § 606. Effect of presumption affecting burden of proof
The effect of a presumption affecting the burden of proof is to impose upon the party against whom it operates the burden of proof as to the nonexistence of the presumed fact.

C.E.C. § 607. Effect of certain presumptions in a criminal action
When a presumption affecting the burden of proof operates in a criminal action to establish presumptively any fact that is essential to the defendant's guilt, the presumption operates only if the facts that give rise to the presumption have been found or otherwise established beyond a reasonable doubt and, in such case, the defendant need only raise a reasonable doubt as to the existence of the presumed fact.

C.E.C. § 620. Conclusive presumptions
The presumptions established by this article, and all other presumptions declared

by law to be conclusive, are conclusive presumptions.

C.E.C. § 630. Presumptions affecting the burden of producing evidence

The presumptions established by this article, and all other rebuttable presumptions established by law that fall within the criteria of Section 603, are presumptions affecting the burden of producing evidence.

C.E.C. § 660. Presumptions affecting the burden of proof

The presumptions established by this article, and all other rebuttable presumptions established by law that fall within the criteria of Section 605, are presumptions affecting the burden of proof.

Questions for Classroom Discussion
Casebook page 621

1. Does the C.E.C. treat all presumptions as having the same effect? If not, why not?

2. Action by Plaintiff, beneficiary of a life insurance policy in the name of Alpha, against the insurer, for failure to pay the benefits under the policy. The insurer refused to pay because it asserts that Alpha is still alive. To prove Alpha is dead, Plaintiff offers evidence that nobody has heard from Alpha in five years. C.E.C. § 667 provides: "A person not heard from in five years is presumed to be dead." The presumption falls into the category of "presumptions affecting the burden of proof." What is the effect of the presumption under the C.E.C.? Would the effect be different if the Federal Rules applied?

CALIFORNIA CONSTITUTION
ARTICLE 1, SECTION 28
(The Victims' Bill of Rights")

§ 28. Legislative findings and declaration; rights of victims; restitution; safe schools; truth-in-evidence; bail; prior convictions

(a) Legislative findings and declaration; rights of victims. The People of the State of California find and declare that the enactment of comprehensive provisions and laws ensuring a bill of rights for victims of crime, including safeguards in the criminal justice system to fully protect those rights, is a matter of grave statewide concern. ...

To accomplish these goals, broad reforms in the procedural treatment of accused persons and the disposition and sentencing of convicted persons are necessary and proper as deterrents to criminal behavior and to serious disruption of people's lives. ...

(d) Right to Truth-in-Evidence. Except as provided by statute hereafter enacted by a two-thirds vote of the membership in each house of the Legislature, relevant evidence shall not be excluded in any criminal proceeding, including pretrial and post conviction motions and hearings, or in any trial or hearing of a juvenile for a criminal offense, whether heard in juvenile or adult court. Nothing in this section shall affect any existing statutory rule of evidence relating to privilege or hearsay, or Evidence Code, Sections 352, 782 or 1103. Nothing in this section shall affect any existing statutory or constitutional right of the press. ...

(f) Use of Prior Convictions. Any prior felony conviction of any person in any criminal proceeding, whether adult or juvenile, shall subsequently be used without limitation for purposes of impeachment or enhancement of sentence in any criminal proceeding. When a prior felony conviction is an element of any felony offense, it shall be proven to the trier of fact in open court.

(Added by Initiative Measure, approved by the people June 8, 1982.)